The
BARNABAS FACTOR

Realize Your
Encouragement Potential

The

BARNABAS FACTOR

Realize Your
Encouragement
Potential

Aubrey Johnson

Gospel Advocate Company • *Nashville, Tennessee*

W9-BPJ-153

Published by Gospel Advocate Co.
1006 Elm Hill Pike, Nashville, TN 37210
http://www.gospeladvocate.com

ISBN: 0-89225-538-2

Dedication

To my father-in-law and mother-in-law,
Gale and Marge Hearn, exceptional encouragers
in the faith of our Lord and Savior Jesus Christ.

The Encourager's Prayer

Dear Father, thank You for a new day
and the opportunities it will afford me to encourage someone in
  Your name.
Thank You for helping me overcome my fears
by giving me a spirit of power and of love and of a sound mind.
Thank You for helping me overcome discouragement
by reminding me of Your unlimited power and abiding presence.
Thank You for helping me live courageously and relate effectively.

Teach me to use my mind to encourage others
by focusing on solutions rather than complaining or assigning
  blame.
Teach me to use my eyes to encourage others
by looking for good in every person and circumstance.
Teach me to use my ears to encourage others
by being quick to hear, slow to speak, and slow to wrath.
Teach me to use my lips to encourage others
by speaking words of hope and healing.
Teach me to use my hands to encourage others
by doing small deeds of kindness expecting nothing in return.

Today, Lord, I will help someone to build
by nudging her one step closer to her dreams.
Today, Lord, I will help someone to blossom
by refusing to give up on him no matter how low he has fallen.
Today, Lord, I will help someone to believe
by showing her she is valuable, loveable and capable.
Today, Lord, I will help someone to battle
by urging him to face his fears instead of running away.
Today, Lord, I will glorify You
through my ministry of encouragement.

— Aubrey Johnson

Table *of* Contents

Foreword

---

*"Those who are lifting the world upward and onward
are those who encourage more than criticize."*

Elizabeth Harrison

To a world characterized by dysfunctional society, fractured families
and churches, and disillusioned individuals, *The Barnabas Factor*
offers a powerful yet practical guide to hope and confidence. The reader will find this book a challenging and exciting study of long-ignored
biblical principles that offer solutions to real and current problems. It
addresses the sense of nagging disappointment – or even hopelessness
that afflict even many Christians and provides a plan for immediate
action. It reminds the reader that the God of creation and destiny has
provided His children both the example and instruction needed for
victorious living.

Through careful biblical scholarship and refreshing insights into
God's provision for man's need for encouragement and to encourage,
the book is suitable for both individual and class study. The story of
Barnabas in the early church provides a concrete example of the attitude, anatomy and activity of an encourager. The passion of the pres-
entation touches heart and mind with a vision of what can be done to
rescue lives from doubt, loneliness and fear.

The world into which Christianity came rivaled the present age in shameful behavior, brutality and despair-filled lives. The Roman Empire ruled the known world with an arrogance of power and a total disregard for the well being of its subjects. It seemed impossible for the teaching of a Jew in obscure Galilee to penetrate its armor of wealth and power. And yet, from the example, faith and death-defying conviction of the early Christians came a greater power that in time brought the overthrow of mighty Rome.

How could this happen? It has been said that those who followed the path of the lowly Nazarene out-thought the pagan world, out-lived the pagan world, and out-died the pagan world. Who would have thought that the encouragement of a crucified Nazarene could inspire such devotion, steadfastness and victorious living and dying? His example and teaching make clear the power available to us through the application of the principles set forth in *The Barnabas Factor*.

In addition to an encouraging text, each lesson contains topics and questions to help the reader make specific applications to life. There is a "Living Like Barnabas" checklist to help pinpoint successes or failures during the previous week.

Such sentiments as the following offer much-needed direction for the future: "A person's life is the result of two things: vision and labor. The greater one's vision and the greater one's labor, the greater one's life. Achievement is not a matter of fate or chance. It is the product of high ideals and heroic endeavor. ... Courageous living is a life of high character; of making, using and adapting to circumstances of noble achievements accomplished through holy ambition and hard work. It is also a life of calmness. Nothing epitomizes encouragement more than poise under pressure. Composure is the crown of a completed character."

"For without belittling the courage with which men have died, we should not forget those acts of courage with which men...have lived. The courage of life is often a less dramatic spectacle than the courage of a final moment; but it is no less a magnificent mixture of triumph and tragedy. A man does what he must – in spite of personal consequences, in spite of obstacles and dangers and pressures – and that is the basis of all human morality."

PRESIDENT JOHN F. KENNEDY

What Is the
Barnabas Factor?

*"Don't let life discourage you; everyone who got where he is
had to begin where he was."*

Richard L. Evans

What is the Barnabas factor? It is recognizing the importance of encouragement in human development and utilizing its power to advance spiritual aims. Encouragement is the process of inspiring others to live with greater hope, confidence and determination. People need courage in order to relate well, to accomplish personal and professional goals, and to thrive emotionally and spiritually. This book will familiarize you with the knowledge and skills necessary to maximize your potential as an encourager.

More than anyone in his day, Barnabas understood the value of encouragement for strengthening individuals and churches. His story will be told in Chapter 11, but his spirit will permeate every page of this book. Like Barnabas, those who grasp the relational nature of Christianity and strive to improve their interpersonal skills can expand their influence for the Savior.

The Barnabas Factor is divided into three sections: "The Attitude of an Encourager," "The Anatomy of an Encourager," and "The Activity of an Encourager." To gain the most from this book, it should be read slowly and deliberately. It is a soul-searching study for people who are serious about spiritual growth. May God bless you as you embark on an adventure in personal transformation that will enrich your life forever.

The Attitude of an Encourager

The attitude of an encourager is a spirit of boldness rooted in unquenchable faith. Just as the body without the spirit is dead, so are the dreams of those who lack courage to take action. Only the brave hearted can experience abundant life. This section of the book deals with theory and provides an understanding of the inner workings of encouragement that will serve as a foundation for the rest of the study.

The Anatomy of an Encourager

The anatomy of an encourager refers to the tools of this biblical ministry. Encouragement requires the wholehearted investment of every human faculty. These practical lessons focus on developing five essential skills for effectively relating to others and achieving your dreams.

The Activity of an Encourager

The activity of an encourager involves the combination and consistent application of knowledge and skill. The goal is to make living courageously and encouraging others second nature. This section of the book is motivational and designed to spur you to action by relating inspirational stories of great encouragers practicing their craft.

The
Attitude

of an
Encourager

Encouragement Is a Biblical Ministry

*"Whether you be man or woman you will never
do anything in this world without courage."*

JAMES LANE ALLEN

Human beings are social creatures instilled by God with an innate desire to spend time with other people. That is why isolation is such a powerful form of punishing antisocial behavior. Disruptive prisoners are placed in solitary confinement. Disobedient children are sent to their rooms. Although everyone has an occasional need to be alone, prolonged isolation can be psychologically painful or even damaging.

When people come together, they have a lasting influence on those with whom they interact. Whether that influence is helpful or hurtful depends on the development and utilization of encouragement skills. Encouragers are people who are unusually effective in relating to others in a positive way. They are pleasant to be around because of their optimism and enthusiasm about life. They radiate a quiet self-confidence which enables them to focus on others rather than demanding constant attention to fulfill their emotional needs.

Encouragement builds healthy self-esteem. It enables people to live with themselves despite their human frailties and imperfections. At the same time, it provides the power needed to make significant changes in personality and behavior. The goal is not self-satisfaction but self-acceptance during a lifetime of spiritual growth.

Encouragers make excellent friends, endearing family members, and highly productive employees. They also are extremely effective as Christians. Christianity is a relationship religion, and encouragement is the chief element in all good personal relationships.

Godly Encouragers From the Past

Encouragement is more than a trend in popular psychology. It is a biblical ministry. In addition to direct commands to encourage (1 Thessalonians 5:11; Hebrews 3:13), the Bible provides numerous examples of godly men and women practicing this spiritual art. Moses, for instance, was commanded by God to encourage Joshua who was about to take his place as national leader of Israel.

> Go up to the top of Pisgah, and lift your eyes toward the west, the north, the south, and the east; behold it with your eyes, for you shall not cross over this Jordan. But command Joshua, and encourage him and strengthen him; for he shall go over before this people, and he shall cause them to inherit the land which you will see (Deuteronomy 3:27-28).

Hezekiah spoke reassuring words to the discouraged people of Jerusalem during the siege of the city by the Assyrian King Sennacharib.

> Then he set military captains over the people, gathered them together to him in the open square of the city gate, and gave them encouragement, saying, "Be strong and courageous; do not be afraid nor dismayed before the king of Assyria, nor before all the multitude that is with him; for there are more with us than with him. With him is an arm of flesh; but with us is the LORD our God, to help us and to fight our battles." And the people were strengthened by the words of Hezekiah king of Judah (2 Chronicles 32:6-8).

Paul was one of the greatest encouragers in New Testament times. Even in jail, he continually looked for opportunities to lift people's spirits. Most notable was his letter-writing ministry to churches in Ephesus, Philippi and Colosse.

> For I want you to know what a great conflict I have for you
> and those in Laodicea, and for as many as have not seen
> my face in the flesh, that their hearts may be encouraged,
> being knit together in love, and attaining to all riches of
> the full assurance of understanding, to the knowledge of
> the mystery of God, both of the Father and of Christ
> (Colossians 2:1-2).

Scripture is filled with inspirational stories of men and women en-gaging in the ministry of encouragement. Just the mention of names such as David and Deborah gives hope to the weary. Prophets like Elijah and Elisha urged their countrymen to maintain a covenant re-lationship with God. The psalmists cheered the hearts of worshipers by centering their thoughts on the goodness and greatness of the Lord. The apostles devoted their lives to dispensing good news of forgive-ness and abundant life in Christ. Clearly, the Bible was written and preserved as a source of encouragement for all ages.

Encouragers Needed Today

Yet never has the need for encouragement been greater than today. Watching the evening news, one quickly gets a sense that man's search for meaning and happiness has been misguided and unsatisfying. That trend is especially evident among America's youth. The rate of at-tempted suicide among teens is an indication that they are deeply dis-couraged. Gang involvement is another clear cry for help. If adoles-cents do not receive attention and support from parents, they will find it among peers. They desperately want to feel a sense of belonging and to know they matter to others. That desire to belong is so strong that young people will place themselves in great personal jeopardy to sat-isfy it. Numerous types of risky or self-destructive behavior are relat-ed to a lack of encouragement.

Hopelessness is by no means limited to the hormone-driven ado-lescent years. Adults frequently exhibit despondency in unhealthful practices such as alcoholism and adultery. In most cases, discourage-ment does not lead to sinful or embarrassing behavior, but it is in-variably disruptive to any sense of normalcy in daily life.

The media makes its living by spotlighting extreme examples of human despair, but discouragement can also take milder, less newsworthy forms. Perhaps the most common evidences of hopelessness are garden-variety depression (feeling down-in-the-dumps) and negative attitudes about the ability to change. Far from innocuous, these beliefs and emotions lead to self-defeating habits that mire people in despondency. Over time, what may appear to be a harmless case of the blues or low self-esteem can ravage a person's ability to function and enjoy life.

Human Magnets

People need and desire encouragement regardless of their sex, social status or stage in life. Whether confronting a personal problem or celebrating an accomplished goal, what kind of individuals do people seek out with whom to share their joys and sorrows? Do they search for pessimists and prophets of doom? Do they long to talk with critics and cynics? No, they look for people with a special talent to encourage.

Encouragers clearly bring out the best in others, but what is it that makes them so likeable? The attraction can be traced back to a pattern of behavior that all encouragers have in common. They listen in a way that makes people feel understood. They are patient and slow to judge. Encouragers take time for others and make them feel special. They rejoice in people's personal victories and are sincerely excited for them. Because discouragers lack these qualities, their personalities tend to drive others away rather than draw them closer.

A Matter of Choice

Although the terms "encouragement" and "discouragement" are relative in nature, it is true that every human being will fall more or less into one of these two categories. It is not possible to be all of one and none of the other, but the goal should be to gravitate toward becoming more of an encourager. Like the stock market, everyone will have ups and downs, good moments and bad ones, but each should strive to move in a more positive direction with the passing of time.

Whenever two people come in contact with each other, they will never be the same. After any encounter, they leave either more encouraged or more discouraged. The good news is that you can consciously choose the impact you will have on those with whom you spend time. That is possible because God has provided human beings with the power to make constructive changes in their lives. Becoming a more encouraging person is simply a matter of choice.

Personal growth is more likely to occur in a supportive atmosphere, and encouragers are committed to providing that kind of nurturing environment. The encourager's ministry is to help people believe in the possibility of improving their character and circumstances with God's help. The encourager's wares are hope and faith, and they are freely dispensed at every opportunity.

Becoming an Encourager

This study is about becoming an encouraging person. That process involves the same steps one would employ in developing skills in any life endeavor. First comes the need for knowledge. Chapters 1 through 4 of this book are dedicated to helping readers understand the dynamics of encouragement. Second comes the practical matter of mastering the skills necessary to be an effective encourager. Chapters 5 through 9 will highlight five basic skills needed to achieve this goal. The final section provides incentive to take action. Chapters 10 through 13 contain motivational examples of encouragers at work. These inspiring stories were selected to help readers begin exercising their own abilities as encouragers.

If you want to become a more encouraging person, the time to start is now. This book will focus on concrete attitudes and actions that, through continual use, will help you achieve lasting personal transformation. Striving to become a more encouraging person is one of life's most enjoyable and rewarding experiences. Do you want to live life more courageously? Do you want to relate to others more effectively? Then let the adventure begin!

THINKING LIKE BARNABAS

1. Why is isolation effective in discouraging antisocial behavior?

2. Why is it possible for encouragers to focus more on others than themselves?

3. How can becoming more encouraging help a person be a better friend?

4. How can encouragement help a person be a better family member?

5. How can becoming more encouraging help a person be a better employee?

6. How can becoming more encouraging help a person be a better Christian?

7. Is encouragement a biblical ministry?

8. Why do all people need encouragement?

9. Can people really change for the better?

10. How do you think becoming more encouraging will help you personally?

BEHAVING LIKE BARNABAS

1. Break into groups and make a list of the traits that are possessed by encouragers and discouragers. Discuss your findings.

2. Pray for this quarter to be a time of personal transformation for each class member.

3. This week's assignment is to encourage a relative other than your spouse or children. Come to next week's class prepared to share your experience.

Something that encouraged me last week was ...

Someone I encouraged last week was ...

To become more encouraging this week, I plan to ...

In the past week, I became more or less discouraging in these areas:

- *Insensitivity*   more / less   (*critical, sarcastic, negative*)

- *Intimidation*   more / less   (*bossy, overbearing, threatening*)

- *Ignoring*   more / less   (*preoccupied, aloof, self-centered*)

On a scale of 1 to 10, my use of encouragement skills during the past week was as follows:

- *My mind*   *1 2 3 4 5 6 7 8 9 10*
  (*thinking good, pure, positive thoughts*)

- *My eyes*   *1 2 3 4 5 6 7 8 9 10*
  (*perceiving the good in every situation*)

- *My ears*   *1 2 3 4 5 6 7 8 9 10*
  (*actively and enthusiastically listening*)

- *My lips*   *1 2 3 4 5 6 7 8 9 10*
  (*verbally communicating respect and confidence*)

- *My hands*   *1 2 3 4 5 6 7 8 9 10*
  (*sensing and acting on opportunities to do good*)

I began each day asking for God's help to become a more encouraging person.
  Yes   *No*

The Power of
Courage

*"Courage is not the absence of fear, but rather the judgment
that something else is more important than fear."*

AMBROSE REDMOON

In his second letter to Timothy, Paul made the marvelous declaration that "God has not given us a spirit of fear, but of power and of love and of a sound mind" (2 Timothy 1:7). Paul understood that much of the dysfunctional behavior he observed in society could be attributed to a lack of courage needed to face life's challenges effectively. The kind of fear that causes emotional paralysis and disables people from moving forward productively with their lives does not come from God. To the contrary, He is the one who provides the spiritual power that equips people to handle any difficulty that comes their way.

It is important not to confuse courage with recklessness. Those who enjoy taking risks are better classified as thrill seekers rather than courageous. One pursues a higher good, the other a good high (albeit natural). Courage is the inner capacity that enables a person to move ahead toward meaningful goals and objectives in life. It is not the absence of fear but the stamina to continue on course despite potentially debilitating fears.

The Bible is filled with accounts of men and women whose faith and courage helped them overcome great obstacles in life. Before entering Canaan, Moses charged Joshua and the Israelites, "Be strong and of good courage, do not fear nor be afraid of them; for the Lord your God, He is the One who goes with you. He will not leave you nor forsake you" (Deuteronomy 31:6). Moses knew that an awareness of God's abiding presence would kindle Joshua's courage. A sense of God's closeness still ignites courage in believers today.

Daniel is a classic example of courage rooted in a right relationship with God. When he was taken captive to Babylon by Nebuchadnezzar, he grappled with many fears while adjusting to his new life. Daniel refused to be dominated by despair. Maintaining a covenant relationship with God was his top priority and the key to his future success. He endeavored to act consistently with his religious beliefs regardless of the consequences.

Within this framework of faith, Daniel aggressively pursued educational and career goals that most Jews felt were beyond their reach. Because of this courage, he advanced to become ruler of the greatest nation on earth (Daniel 2:48). That fortitude won him the respect and admiration of his peers and the leaders of two world empires. Courage made him a man of character and caused him to prosper in all that he did.

Courage is a divine resource needed by all people. It is not reserved for prophets or police officers. The lives of ordinary people may not be as glamorous as those in high risk or high profile occupations, but their need for strength to deal with day-to-day struggles is no less real. It takes courage to discipline children in a permissive society. It takes resolve to decline lucrative job opportunities that infringe on family life. It takes nerve to seek fulfillment as a homemaker in a liberated world.

Courageous men and women endure, bear up, tough it out, and keep on keeping on. They pursue personal ambitions and commitments when others have compromised their dreams and values. Courage is what it takes to follow through on goals despite hardships or difficulties. It enables students to study when they would prefer to play. It empowers athletes to work out when they would like to sleep in. It inspires dieters to eat sensibly when they would rather indulge. Impressive displays of courage are exhibited every day in the lives of regular people.

More than anyone else, Christians should recognize that courage is needed on a daily basis. What should a person do when asked by the boss to falsify information on insurance forms? How does a saint respond to group pressure to participate in immoral or unethical behavior?

It takes backbone to walk down an aisle and request baptism or the prayers of the congregation. It requires boldness for a Christian to share his faith with friends and co-workers. It takes mettle to contend for the faith against false teaching. Courage makes it possible for an individual to stand up for what he believes even when it is unpopular.

The difference between courage and fear is in the direction. Courage implies positive, forward movement. Fear suggests negative movement or the failure to move at all. Courage is progress, and fear is paralysis. Both are based on one's attitudes, beliefs and expectations.

Attitudes

There are two ways to handle life's difficulties: the easy way of shortcuts and compromises or the courageous way of conviction and perseverance. How one chooses to respond to adversity can usually be traced back to attitude. A fearful person looks at the problems until they seem insurmountable. A courageous person looks at the possibilities until they seem reachable. Courage and fear are a matter of focus.

Attitudes dramatically influence performance. Those who are discouraged are more likely to focus on perceptions of their personal limitations that are overblown. If a person believes that others are more competent or better connected, he is likely to perform more poorly than if he feels good about himself. Negative beliefs, however inaccurate, almost inevitably steer a person on a self-defeating course. Courageous people have confidence in their ability to cope with any circumstance. In the darkest situations, they see light at the end of the tunnel. They are never without hope.

Beliefs

Faith is courage enhancing. When the terrified disciples woke the Lord during a storm on the Sea of Galilee, He said to them, "Why are you fearful, O you of little faith" (Matthew 8:26). Faith dispels fear and imparts courage. The psalmist wrote, "Whenever I am afraid, I will trust in You" (Psalm 56:3).

Faith operates by establishing a proper belief system. Through faith in God, Christians can rejoice even when problems arise. Courageous people expect adversity and perceive it as an opportunity to demonstrate faith and grow spiritually (James 1:1-12). They are confident of God's presence in the midst of crisis and certain that His grace will be sufficient to sustain them. Believers are sure that no problem is bigger than their ability to bear it (1 Corinthians 10:13).

Christians are able to live courageously because of their faith in God's promises contained in the Bible. They recall the words of the angel Gabriel who proclaimed that nothing is impossible for God (Luke 1:37). They remember the words of Paul who assured believers they can do all things though the strength Christ affords them (Philippians 4:13). These convictions enable saints to live effectively in prosperity and adversity. The power that provides the positive direction for their lives is not derived from self-reliance but from confidence in God.

Faulty beliefs, on the other hand, have the potential to diminish courage. Who can calculate the emotional price one pays for doubting the existence or love of God? Many lesser misconceptions are held on a subconscious level, and people are unaware of the extent to which their daily lives are controlled by them. Consider these examples:

• Everybody must like me (nobody likes me).
• Everyone must agree with me (nobody understands me).
• Things must go my way (I never get my way).
• There is only one right solution (nothing can fix this mess).
• Life must be fair at all times (I always get a raw deal).

Notice the tendency to exaggerate and to universalize negative beliefs. Those who accept such ideas become emotionally crippled and lack the capacity to meet challenges and achieve goals. They are out of touch with reality and unwilling to take responsibility for their lives. Nothing can change for the better until they change the way they think.

Expectations

Anticipation is the third ingredient necessary for courageous living. It provides fearlessness to carry on in the face of great difficulties because of confidence in the final outcome. Encouragers believe that the very struggle to persevere is the most satisfying and rewarding approach to life. They are convinced there is more to be gained by endurance than instability and by bravery than cowardice (Matthew 16:25).

In most cases, people perform in keeping with their expectations of themselves. Lack of drive and determination are often the result of self-doubt. The discouraged person unconsciously reasons, "Why do my best if failure is inevitable?" The prospect of failure (and the overly broad definition of the term) becomes a self-fulfilling prophecy by producing a less than earnest attempt doomed from the outset. Anticipating failure sets in motion a negative chain of events from which it is difficult to recover. When a person does not exercise courage, he loses some of his spiritual spunk. By acting fearlessly, he is energized. Effort and expectations are inseparably linked.

Partners

Courage alone is insufficient for successful living. It is merely the quality that undergirds one's values. It helps people to follow their beliefs and move in the direction of their fulfillment, but it does not guarantee a proper belief system. A person can have the courage of his convictions and yet be wrong.

When biblical values are understood and accepted, courage will support them in action. Courage is the partner of the conscience. When a person struggles with competing values, courage stimulates support for doing what one believes is more virtuous, healthful and constructive. It inspires man's highest ideals and strengthens his resolve to act in accordance with them. Courage kindles the heart's warmest impulses and prods a person to act upon them before the embers of incentive cool.

Courage enabled Abraham to heed God's call and move his family from the metropolis of Ur to live as tent dwellers in a strange land. It was courage that empowered Noah to build an ark amid the taunts of townspeople who could not envision the coming flood promised by God. Courage gave David the confidence he needed to fight the Philistines' champion in the valley of Elah.

It was a shortage of courage that caused Aaron to give in to the mob's demand to fashion new gods for Israel. Pilate displayed a deficiency of determination when he allowed Jesus to be crucified although he knew He was innocent. When people do wrong, they usually know better. To know better than one does often indicates a lack of courage needed to follow through on convictions. By affirming positive attitudes, beliefs and expectations, people are more likely to act in keeping with their consciences.

Jesus is the ultimate example of courageous living. Busy pursuing His dreams, He refused to be deterred by obstacles or opposition. Although threatened, reviled and attacked, He remained focused on His goals. Not even death threats could alter His course. Jesus is an encouraging model of how life can be lived at its very best.

Those who were closest to Jesus and personally trained by Him had mixed results in their own attempts to live courageously. Peter, for example, experienced times of great boldness and times of great disappointment. He would bravely walk on water, then sink in fear. In the garden, he defended the Master, but in the courtyard, he denied Him. He proclaimed that Gentiles had a right to fellowship in the kingdom, but he denied them his fellowship in a common meal.

The Heart and Soul of Encouragement

Like Peter, modern Christians will find that some days they behave with more courage than others. That is why there is a real need among the people of God for the courage to be imperfect. Self-satisfaction and self-abhorrence are mortal enemies of courage. Self-acceptance, on the other hand, promotes good mental and spiritual health when accompanied with a strong desire to grow spiritually.

Courage is the heart and soul of encouragement. When activated, it enables ordinary people to uphold their convictions and accomplish their dreams. By overcoming bad attitudes, mistaken beliefs, and negative expectations, you can begin living courageously. In the next two lessons, a closer examination will be made of what depletes and replenishes a person's supply of courage.

THINKING LIKE BARNABAS

1. How would you define "courage"?

2. What is the difference between courage and recklessness?

Something that encouraged me last week was …

Someone I encouraged last week was …

To become more encouraging this week, I plan to …

In the past week, I became more or less discouraging in these areas:

- Insensitivity   more / less   (critical, sarcastic, negative)

- Intimidation   more / less   (bossy, overbearing, threatening)

- Ignoring   more / less   (preoccupied, aloof, self-centered)

On a scale of 1 to 10, my use of encouragement skills during the past week was as follows:

- My mind   1 2 3 4 5 6 7 8 9 10
(thinking good, pure, positive thoughts)

- My eyes   1 2 3 4 5 6 7 8 9 10
(perceiving the good in every situation)

- My ears   1 2 3 4 5 6 7 8 9 10
(actively and enthusiastically listening)

- My lips   1 2 3 4 5 6 7 8 9 10
(verbally communicating respect and confidence)

- My hands   1 2 3 4 5 6 7 8 9 10
(sensing and acting on opportunities to do good)

I began each day asking for God's help to become a more encouraging person.
    Yes   No

3. Why do ordinary people need courage?

4. Upon what do Christians base their courage?

5. How are courage and fear a matter of focus?

6. How can mistaken beliefs diminish courage?

7. How do expectations impact a person's ability to perform well?

8. Why does a person lose some of his spunk when he fails to exercise courage?

9. How is courage the partner of the conscience?

10. How do Christians need the courage to be imperfect?

BEHAVING LIKE BARNABAS

1. Break into groups and make a list of times when Christians need courage.

2. Ask God for greater courage to keep commitments and accomplish worthwhile goals.

3. This week's assignment is to encourage a friend. Be creative.

The Problem of Discouragement

---

*"God grant me the courage not to give up what
I think is right even though I think it is hopeless."*

ADMIRAL CHESTER W. NIMITZ

D iscouragement is the stage a person has reached when he has consciously or unconsciously decided there is little or no hope. This can be limited to a specific endeavor or one can be totally discouraged about life and the ability to make a meaningful contribution to it. When people feel this way, they either anticipate failure, which causes them to perform poorly, or they simply give up, despairing of any chance to succeed.

Hopelessness is usually a mistaken perception. The problem is an inability to see the possible choices for making positive change in one's situation. Discouragement is the result of a flawed focus.

Discouraged people frequently do not like themselves and can be overheard mumbling self-directed put-downs. In reality, they are prone to overemphasize their human imperfections and to overreact whenever they make a mistake. They are uneasy accepting praise but quick to internalize criticism. Disheartened people are often lonely because their pessimism results in an unpleasant personality that drives others away. Seeing themselves as victims, they are more likely to turn to artificial forms of courage like alcohol to find relief from their loneliness and pain.

A discouraged person perceives life as unfair. He believes success and failure are more a result of circumstance than stamina or of fate than fortitude. He constantly compares himself to others because he considers life a never ending battle measured in wins and losses. Status and prestige become matters of excessive concern.

Problems are considered devastating crises rather than challenges or opportunities. The depressed person lacks confidence in his ability to handle adversity successfully. He believes that the odds are stacked against him and that nothing will ever change.

The courageous person, on the other hand, accepts who he is without being limited by it. He is not controlled by an obsession to compare and compete. He accepts his circumstances as how things are but not as they have to be. This provides the foundation to begin positive movement despite existing difficulties.

Common Causes of Discouragement

Two of the most common causes of discouragement are misfortunes and mistakes. Although trials are a normal part of life, lack of courage can cause a person to despair when they are encountered. Injury and illness can be emotionally overwhelming. Divorce or the death of a loved one can be totally devastating. Unfulfilled dreams are like sores that will not heal. Lack of appreciation can break a person's spirit. Weariness with simple day-to-day stress can lead to burn out. Overcommitment can cause mental and physical fatigue that drag a person down.

• *Misfortunes.* Joseph was a man whose courage enabled him to withstand severe trials. He had every reason to be discouraged but remained undaunted. When sold into slavery by his brothers, he did not mope and sulk. When he was cast into prison for resisting the advances of Potiphar's wife, he did not waste time brooding. When circumstances were beyond his control, he made the best of them. Unable to change his conditions, he changed his attitude.

No matter how bad things became, Joseph never lost hope. He accepted his plight but never stopped working to improve his situation. His life epitomized the proverb "Bloom where you are planted." His faith in God's ability to bring good out of evil was vindicated when he became second in command to Pharaoh. The position he providentially acquired allowed him to save his family from starvation during a regional famine. Yet, regardless of the outcome, encouragers believe that life is happier and more satisfying when lived courageously.

• **Mistakes.** Mistakes (and intentional wrongdoing) can also diminish a person's supply of courage. Errors in judgment can lead to job termination, incarceration, and serious health problems. A person who violates his conscience can experience destructive feelings of guilt and shame. One ought to be remorseful for wrongdoing, but not hopeless. He should feel sad, but not despair. He should be penitent, but not defeated.

Judas is a prime example of a person who was discouraged because of a bad decision. His crime was disloyalty. He betrayed a close friend, and his conscience was unable to bear the enormous weight of guilt that ensued. The use of a kiss to double cross Jesus seemed brilliant at first, but in the end, it was an agonizing memory he could not endure. Judas never imagined the mental anguish his treachery would bring. Desperate to end his suffering, he committed suicide by hanging himself.

There is no doubt that Judas committed a grievous sin, but were things really as hopeless as they seemed? Was death the only way out? Discouragement blinded him to constructive choices for dealing with his offense. God loved Judas despite his treachery, and Jesus died to forgive his sin. Judas was simply too discouraged to envision the grace and forgiveness that were available to him through repentance.

Peter, who denied his Lord under oath, was in a situation very similar to Judas. Both had betrayed Jesus, and both were remorseful, but Peter never lost hope. The difference was courage. Judas allowed his mistake to overwhelm him. Peter regretted his behavior, but refused to let it destroy him. He received God's forgiveness and, because of his experience, became more sensitive to the personal failings of others.

Unintentional Discouragement

In addition to the things a person may do to discourage himself, there are three ways people unintentionally discourage others – through insensitivity, intimidation and negligence.

• **Insensitivity.** Encouragers have a tender side that helps them empathize with people's feelings. Discouragers mean well but are oblivious to the pain they inflict.

Criticism is the most prevalent form of insensitivity. What one person considers helpful advice may be devastating to the person on the other end. It only takes an instant for critics to drain a person of drive. Like a pin that bursts a balloon, hurtful words can puncture the pride and self-esteem of an insecure person. The source of censorship may be an unreasonable boss, an overbearing spouse, impossible to please in-laws, or perfectionist parents. The unreasonable standards of other people can make a person feel inferior or incompetent. The last thing a discouraged person needs is criticism.

Encouragement helps to ward off the effects of destructive criticism. Nehemiah faced many critics when he came from Persia to rebuild Jerusalem's walls. There was no shortage of people to point out the obstacles and difficulties he faced. He became the target of a constant barrage of criticism and was repeatedly told why the job could not be done. The Samaritans used mockery and ridicule to demoralize the Jews and their leader.

Somehow, Nehemiah withstood his critics and accomplished his dream where many others had failed. He prayed about his opposition, and kept his focus on the task at hand. The encouragement of this single man negated the deluge of negativity rained upon the builders and gave them the courage to go on. Critics are discouragers who accomplish little that is constructive. Leaders are encouragers who inspire others to achieve positive ends.

Sarcasm is one of the cruelest forms of insensitivity. It is excused as kidding, but the kernel of truth that makes it funny also makes it sting. Too much sarcasm or bad timing can crush a person's feelings and potentially ruin a relationship. Humor is not funny when it harms another person.

• *Intimidation.* Intimidation is another means of siphoning a person's reservoir of courage. There are two senses in which intimidation can demoralize. The first is by browbeating or bullying another person until he is so afraid he can barely function. Bosses, coaches and parents who manage people by threats and harassment delude themselves into believing they are bringing out their best. Influencing by intimidation can rob subordinates of their dignity, and those who do not excel under this crude style of motivation are discarded or made to feel inadequate.

Domination is a variation of intimidation. It is the opposite of brow-beating. In this situation, a person is pampered and protected to an extreme. The unspoken message is that the sheltered individual is incapable. As a result, he never develops coping skills and actually becomes dependent on others.

• *Ignoring.* A final way to dishearten someone is simply to ignore him. Silence can shake a person's self-confidence and deflate his pride. Everyone wants to be noticed and appreciated. When a person feels overlooked, it will either dash his spirits or cause him to seek attention in less than desirable ways. As his attempts to get attention grow more desperate, he becomes increasingly obnoxious. The more he presses, the more he alienates others. His efforts backfire on him and deepen his discouragement.

Defeating Discouragement

If insensitivity, intimidation and ignoring are ways to inhibit personal growth, then they can also provide insight into ways to encourage. Rather than criticize, compliment. Rather than browbeat, express belief. Establish realistic standards for others' performance and affirm your confidence in their ability to function well. Instead of shielding, equip others with the tools and confidence needed to succeed. Instead of neglecting or overlooking people, acknowledge and appreciate them. When people are supported in these simple ways, their courage is replenished. Instead of emotionally wilting, they thrive and grow.

• *Faith.* Christians have been provided with powerful weapons to defeat discouragement, and none is more potent than faith in God. When a person discovers he was made in God's image and that Christ loved him enough to die for his sins, he cannot help being encouraged. By virtue of creation and the cross, human beings have intrinsic worth. Faith imparts security, grants meaning to human existence, puts problems into perspective, and fills the heart with hope. Trust is the substance that transforms Christians into "eternal" optimists.

• *Prayer.* Prayer is a second resource in times of discouragement. God asks His people to unload all their cares upon Him with full assurance that He hears, understands and acts in their behalf (1 Peter 5:7). He promises to bring good out of evil when adversity is met by faith (Romans 8:28). He pledges to provide strength to overcome any temptation (2 Corinthians 12:7-10). He guarantees to bestow peace that passes understanding (Philippians 4:6-7). Prayer is an encourager's first recourse in times of trouble.

• **Fellowship.** A third armament to ward off discouragement is fellowship with the people of God. The church is a loving family that acts as a support group for the discouraged. Its assemblies are a place of refuge where courage can be replenished to return and confront a disheartening world. Faith, prayer and Christian friends are among heaven's resources to defeat despair.

A Journey of Discouragement

The book of Numbers contains a noteworthy example of discouragement from the early history of the Hebrews. As they traveled from Mount Sinai to Canaan, the journey was so difficult that Moses commented, "the soul of the people became very discouraged on the way" (Numbers 21:4). When they finally arrived near their destination, Moses sent out 12 spies to bring back a description of the land. Moses summed up the majority report by saying, "they discouraged the heart of the children of Israel, so that they did not go into the land which the Lord had given them" (32:9). The Jews attempted to justify their disobedience by shifting the blame to the spies. They said, "Where can we go up? Our brethren have discouraged our hearts" (Deuteronomy 1:28). Moses identified the real problem when he said, "you did not believe the Lord" (v. 32).

Only two men did not succumb to discouragement. Joshua and Caleb scouted the land and saw the same giants, the same armies and the same fortifications as the other spies. They heard the disheartening report of their peers and were fully aware of the obstacles to be overcome. Why were they so confident the land could be conquered? The difference was their faith. Belief in God bolstered their courage and gave them a unique frame of reference. Consequently, they were able to search for solutions rather than bemoan the difficulties. Faith focused their attention on God's strength rather than their weakness.

Mistaken beliefs halted the progress of the majority, but trust in God opened up endless possibilities for the faithful. Modern Joshuas and Calebs are the movers and shakers of the church and society.

The Devil's Device

Discouragement is the devil's device to deprive saints of heart and hope. In order for discouragement to succeed, he must persuade people to focus on the negative, expect failure and accept faulty beliefs. Satan enjoys his job and is quite good at it, but Christians find far greater joy in fulfilling their mission as encouragers. Every saint should be committed to developing competence in imparting faith and hope to those in need.

Discouragement is a heart attack in the truest sense. Just as the physical heart pumps life giving blood to every extremity of the body, so those who are courageous in heart have a steady supply of faith that reaches every facet of their lives. When a blockage occurs, hope will die unless the flow of faith can be restored. Encouragement is the healing art of the human heart.

THINKING LIKE BARNABAS

1. How would you define "discouragement"?

2. Why is hopelessness a mistaken belief?

3. Why are discouraged people quicker to internalize criticism than praise?

4. Why are trials more devastating to people when they are discouraged?

5. Did Judas have any options besides suicide? Why couldn't he see them?

6. Describe three common ways people discourage each other. Give examples.

7. What is the difference between browbeating and domination?

8. What weapons are available to battle discouragement?

9. Why does Satan want people discouraged? Does he enjoy his job?

10. How can discouragement be compared to a heart attack?

BEHAVING LIKE BARNABAS

1. Break into groups and make a top 10 list of things that discourage people. Brainstorm first and then prioritize. Discuss how these situations can be handled courageously.

2. Pray for God's help in your daily battle against discouraging beliefs and behavior.

3. This week's assignment is to encourage your spouse. If you are unmarried or widowed, choose a close friend as a substitute.

Something that encouraged me last week was ...

Someone I encouraged last week was ...

To become more encouraging this week, I plan to ...

In the past week, I became more or less discouraging in these areas:

- *Insensitivity*   *more / less*   (*critical, sarcastic, negative*)

- *Intimidation*   *more / less*   (*bossy, overbearing, threatening*)

- *Ignoring*   *more / less*   (*preoccupied, aloof, self-centered*)

On a scale of 1 to 10, my use of encouragement skills during the past week was as follows:

- *My mind*   *1 2 3 4 5 6 7 8 9 10*
(*thinking good, pure, positive thoughts*)

- *My eyes*   *1 2 3 4 5 6 7 8 9 10*
(*perceiving the good in every situation*)

- *My ears*   *1 2 3 4 5 6 7 8 9 10*
(*actively and enthusiastically listening*)

- *My lips*   *1 2 3 4 5 6 7 8 9 10*
(*verbally communicating respect and confidence*)

- *My hands*   *1 2 3 4 5 6 7 8 9 10*
(*sensing and acting on opportunities to do good*)

I began each day asking for God's help to become a more encouraging person.
    Yes   *No*

The Possibilities of Encouragement

Encouragement is the process of inspiring others to live with greater hope and courage. Practically speaking, it is the ability to leave people feeling more positive and confident after interacting with them. When people stand taller, step livelier or smile wider, they have been encouraged. This coveted commodity can change the course of a person's day or his entire destiny.

Encouragement Zones

Encouragement is an asset sorely needed in every sphere of life. At work, the enthusiasm of the first day on the job can quickly wane because of a dominating boss or lack of deserved recognition. At school, a discouraging teacher can deflate a student's ego and cause his or her performance to plunge. At home, the family designed by God as a place of refuge and renewal can be the greatest source of discouragement a person faces.

The local church was intended by God to be mankind's supreme encouragement zone. Christian assemblies are about worshiping, serving and learning, but they are also about belonging. They are places to love and be loved. No worldly institution can encourage the heart, mind and soul like Jesus' church.

But Satan has attempted to counterfeit the atmosphere of the church in numerous secular settings. Many people join service organizations or frequent entertainment establishments searching for a place to belong. For their monthly dues or a night's cover charge, they hope to find something to care about and someone to care about them. They want to talk about their triumphs and troubles and feel someone listens. The church should recognize this universal desire to connect and converse because it alone can offer meaningful answers to what ails mankind. Only the church can provide the encouragement needed to face reality rather than simply talking about it or escaping from it.

Encouragement is essential wherever there are people. The question is, "How can the various realms of life be made into encouragement zones?" The first thing to remember is that people can make the world a more encouraging place only to the extent that they themselves become more encouraging.

Individuals should ask, "How do people feel as a result of being with me? Is my spouse happier because we have been together? Do my children look forward to seeing me? Do co-workers smile when I walk up? Do people come to me to talk about their hopes and dreams or why they are feeling down? Are those I come in contact with able to live their lives more positively and constructively because of our time together?"

Encountering Obstacles

There are plenty of obstacles on the pathway to becoming a more encouraging person.

• *Society's Definition.* Society's proneness to define success in terms of superiority to others is one such hindrance. On this basis, most people are destined to be discouraged despite valuable contributions they make to the world around them. The runner-up in a beauty pageant may think of herself as first among the losers. The fourth place finisher in an Olympic event may feel like a flop because he failed to medal. Middle class Americans, rich by the world's standards, may consider themselves poor because their lifestyles do not compare to their favorite TV star. Unrealistic standards have robbed many people of the happiness and contentment God intended them to enjoy.

• *Seclusion.* Isolation is another roadblock on the road to encouragement. It is difficult for loners to be encouragers because their reclusive lifestyles take them out of circulation. Taking time for others is fundamental to relating effectively. If a person is preoccupied, distant and out of touch, he unconsciously sends the message that the people around him are unimportant in his life. An encourager cannot be selfish or unsociable.

That is why it is critical to attend the services of the church. The mid-week assembly is filled with opportunities to practice the ministry of encouragement. There is real power in fellowship to sustain weary souls in their struggle against worldliness. Handshakes and hugs impart strength. Joining together in prayer and songs of praise affirms faith. The announcements afford countless ministry opportunities that would otherwise be missed. The person who excuses his absence by remarking, "I don't get anything out of it" is saying more about himself than the quality of the service. Mature Christians look forward to each assembly of the church where encouragement is given and received by all who attend.

• *Low Self-Esteem.* A shortage of self-esteem also makes it difficult to relate well to others. Jesus was a great encourager because He felt good about who He was. As a result, He could spend His time building up others rather than promoting Himself.

• *Lack of Experience.* Lack of experience is another significant barrier to encouragement. The ability to encourage is a learned skill that takes plenty of practice. Christians must train themselves in proven techniques for improving their relationships with other people.

• *Inadequate Commitment.* Finally, inadequate commitment will limit one's ability to encourage. Short-term commitments are characteristic of today's culture of instant gratification. Encouragers are dependable people. The ability to stick with relationships and obligations is the underpinning of encouragement.

Essential to Christianity

Encouragement is a legitimate and essential function of Christianity. Plenty of people are ready to tear others down by ridiculing their hopes and dreams. Blessed are the encouragers whose words and deeds sustain the energy, enthusiasm and drive of people attempting to change the world and themselves for the better.

Most biblical injunctions are calls to encourage. The commands to love (Matthew 22:39), to comfort (1 Thessalonians 4:18), and to do good (Galatians 6:10) demand that saints engage in an unending ministry of dispensing hope. Never is a person more Christlike than when he dies to self and allows Christ to live though him in this way. "Encouragement" is a watchword for faithful saints.

People Need Encouragement

Human growth requires more than analysis or advice. People want to know they are valued and that someone believes in them. The goal of encouragement is to help them value and believe in themselves. They need to develop confidence in their abilities and learn how to benefit from mistakes rather than being devastated by them. They need to enjoy compliments and evaluate criticism by using the good without internalizing the bad. They need to develop the capacity to find humor in minor disasters and remain composed in stressful situations.

Human growth requires encouragement. Homes, businesses, schools and churches cannot reach their full potential without it. Parents lacking in basic encouragement skills will limit their child's willingness to take calculated risks that are crucial to full development. Managers incapable of motivating their work force will experience decreased production and company profits. Teachers who cannot inspire will lower students' expectations of themselves and raise their acceptance of mediocrity. Preachers who cannot connect with people will see attendance figures lag and congregational morale dwindle.

Bible school is a classic example of the need for encouragement. Imagine a class where the teacher arrives 15 minutes early and finds all her students present and seated at their desks. Everyone brought a Bible and completed the homework assignment from the previous week. As she speaks, they listen with undivided attention.

Every teacher dreams of a class where no one dozes or daydreams. The fact is that Bible school teachers, like all encouragers, must deal with people where they are, not where they would like them to be.

Imperfect classes should not be a cause of despair. Every display of human frailty merely demonstrates the importance of a teacher's work.

A student in one Bible class wore a sweatshirt emblazoned with the motto, "You can make me go to school, but you can't make me think." Disinterested and disruptive students seem to have that message written upon their hearts. Many young people arrive in the typical Bible class without the slightest intention of learning. What is a teacher to do?

Motivating the Unmotivated

Motivation comes in two forms: intrinsic and extrinsic. If students do not arrive in class already equipped with a desire to learn, it becomes the teacher's job to try and inspire them. The responsibility for what students learn does not rest completely with the teacher, but effective teachers seek to find that internal button that will turn young people on to spiritual truth. Learning has more to do with a student's interest than his intelligence.

How can average adults be transformed into motivational teachers? A director of religious education would suggest creative lesson planning, engaging methods of instruction, and improving the learning environment. Certainly it is true that a teacher half prepared is asking for trouble. Still, a teacher may have the best decorated room and a solid grasp of her lesson yet fail miserably. How can that be? It is because, all things being equal, the teacher who relates best will have the greatest success.

That is not to say that students learn best from the teacher with the most magnetic personality. A teacher who fails to immerse herself in God's Word cannot give what she does not have. Nonetheless, a teacher who is well prepared will multiply her effectiveness by developing encouragement skills. Teaching skills plus encouraging skills equals the most effective Bible teacher.

Students enter a typical Bible school classroom with gnawing hunger pains in their souls. They hunger for love, recognition, affirmation, and respect. It is difficult to teach a child whose stomach is empty but even more difficult to instruct a pupil whose self-esteem is bare. Many children are relationally emaciated. They are overfed and under loved.

It has often been said that to feed the soul, you must first feed the body. Is it equally true that to feed the soul, you must first feed the heart of a child who is starved for attention?

Motivational teachers understand the importance of good relationships with their students. They strive to make personal connections and build emotional bridges. Effective teachers know their pupils as individuals and capitalize on their interests to facilitate learning. They communicate not only facts but also faith in their student's ability to comprehend and internalize the lesson. Encouraging teachers smile often, are generous with their hugs, and praise at every opportunity. There is no higher form of motivation than wanting to please a person who cares about you and believes in you. Love is the greatest encourager.

This classroom principle can be applied to all relationships. Neglected children are more likely to display defiant behavior than those who feel loved. Wise parents, therefore, make great sacrifices to build a strong relationship with their son or daughter.

Managers who are perceived by workers as distant and manipulative are less effective than encouraging ones. Employees who feel their supervisors care about them as people are more likely to be cooperative and productive. Respect for an employee's dignity, integrity and individuality pays rich dividends.

The assembly line approach to conversion is rarely successful. Enthusiastic evangelists must take the time to know individuals they hope to reach for Christ. There is a human element to outreach that must not be ignored.

10 Reminders for Encouragers

1. Remember to encourage others the way you would want to be encouraged in their situation. "Therefore, whatever you want men to do to you, do also to them, for this is the Law and the Prophets" (Matthew 7:12).

2. Remember that people are inclined to treat you the way you treat them. "Give, and it will be given to you: good measure, pressed down, shaken together, and running over will be put into your bosom. For with the same measure that you use, it will be measured back to you" (Luke 6:38).

3. Remember that your time, talent and treasures are heavenly trusts for encouraging others.

[A]ccording to my earnest expectation and hope that in nothing I shall be ashamed, but with all boldness, as always, so now also Christ will be magnified in my body, whether by life or by death. For to me, to live is Christ, and to die is gain. But if I live on in the flesh, this will mean fruit from my labor; yet what I shall choose I cannot tell. For I am hard pressed between the two, having a desire to depart and be with Christ, which is far better. Nevertheless to remain in the flesh is more needful for you. And being confident of this, I know that I shall remain and continue with you all for your progress and joy of faith (Philippians 1:20-25).

4. Remember to prize people above everything except faithfulness to God.

Jesus answered him, "The first of all the commandments is: 'Hear, O Israel, the Lord our God, the Lord is one. And you shall love the Lord your God with all your heart, with all your soul, with all your mind, and with all your strength.' This is the first commandment. And the second, like it, is this: 'You shall love your neighbor as yourself.' There is no other commandment greater than these" (Mark 12:29-31).

5. Remember that every act of encouragement is an act of love for God. "If someone says, 'I love God,' and hates his brother, he is a liar; for he who does not love his brother whom he has seen, how can he love God whom he has not seen? And this commandment we have from Him: that he who loves God must love his brother also" (1 John 4:20-21).

6. Remember that every act of encouragement is an act of love for Christ. "Assuredly, I say to you, inasmuch as you did it to one of the least of these My brethren, you did it to Me" (Matthew 25:40).

7. Remember that one day you must account for every relationship God has placed in your care. "Moreover it is required in stewards that one be found faithful" (1 Corinthians 4:2).

8. Remember that encouraging is a daily privilege and responsibility. "[B]ut exhort one another daily, while it is called 'Today,' lest any of you be hardened through the deceitfulness of sin" (Hebrews 3:13).

9. Remember that God encourages us so that we may encourage others. "Blessed be the God and Father of our Lord Jesus Christ, the Father of mercies and God of all comfort, who comforts us in all our tribulation, that we may be able to comfort those who are in any trouble, with the comfort with which we ourselves are comforted by God" (2 Corinthians 1:3-4).

10. Remember that church assemblies are great opportunities to encourage. "And let us consider one another in order to stir up love and good works, not forsaking the assembling of ourselves together, as is the manner of some, but exhorting one another, and so much the more as you see the Day approaching" (Hebrews 10:24-25).

Ready for the Next Step

Now that you have a better understanding of the dynamics of encouragement, you are well on your way to becoming a more encouraging person. Having the attitude of an encourager has prepared you to take the next step. To reach your full potential as an encourager, you must begin to work on developing the skills necessary to do the job. Section 2 of this book will present those skills in great detail.

THINKING LIKE BARNABAS

1. How would you define "encouragement"?

2. How can you tell if a person has been encouraged?

3. How is defining success in terms of superiority to others discouraging?

4. Why does selfishness limit a person's ability to encourage others?

5. What opportunities to encourage are present at a typical church service?

6. How can low self-esteem make it more difficult to encourage others?

7. How does lack of commitment hinder the ability to encourage?

8. Name some situations where you have observed a need for encouragement.

9. Why is Matthew 7:12 the Golden Rule of all encouragers?

10. What does it mean that Christians are stewards of their relationships?

BEHAVING LIKE BARNABAS

1. Break into groups and come up with your own set of rules for encouragers.

2. Pray for God's help in overcoming the obstacles that hinder encouragement.

3. This week's assignment is to encourage a child. It can be a child at home, a grandchild, a niece or nephew or any other young person. Savor the moment.

Something that encouraged me last week was ...

Someone I encouraged last week was ...

To become more encouraging this week, I plan to ...

In the past week, I became more or less discouraging in these areas:

- *Insensitivity*   *more / less*   (*critical, sarcastic, negative*)

- *Intimidation*   *more / less*   (*bossy, overbearing, threatening*)

- *Ignoring*   *more / less*   (*preoccupied, aloof, self-centered*)

On a scale of 1 to 10, my use of encouragement skills during the past week was as follows:

- My *mind*   1 2 3 4 5 6 7 8 9 10
(*thinking good, pure, positive thoughts*)

- My *eyes*   1 2 3 4 5 6 7 8 9 10
(*perceiving the good in every situation*)

- My *ears*   1 2 3 4 5 6 7 8 9 10
(*actively and enthusiastically listening*)

- My *lips*   1 2 3 4 5 6 7 8 9 10
(*verbally communicating respect and confidence*)

- My *hands*   1 2 3 4 5 6 7 8 9 10
(*sensing and acting on opportunities to do good*)

I began each day asking for God's help to become a more encouraging person.
    Yes   *No*

The
Anatomy

of an
Encourager

The Mind of an Encourager

Organic illness cannot account for all of a person's health problems. Disease and health are often rooted in thought. Fear and anxiety cause numerous digestive and circulatory problems. Guilt can shatter the nervous system. Yet thought can also affect health in a positive way. Cheerful thoughts can enhance the body's natural healing capacities. As Solomon said, "A merry heart does good, like medicine, But a broken spirit dries the bones" (Proverbs 17:22). Holy thoughts can provide serenity to replace destructive stress. There is an undeniable connection between a person's mental and physical well-being.

You Are What You Think

In addition to affecting health, thought can also shape character. Jesus understood the link between thought and integrity and made this lesson an important part of His disciples' training.

> When He had called all the multitude to Himself, He said to them, "Hear Me, everyone, and understand: There is nothing that enters a man from outside which can defile

him; but the things which come out of him, those are the
things that defile a man. If anyone has ears to hear, let him
hear." When He had entered a house away from the crowd,
His disciples asked Him concerning the parable. So He said
to them, "Are you thus without understanding also? Do you
not perceive that whatever enters a man from outside cannot defile him, because it does not enter his heart but his
stomach, and is eliminated, thus purifying all foods?" And
He said, "What comes out of a man, that defiles a man. For
from within, out of the heart of men, proceed evil thoughts,
adulteries, fornications, murders, thefts, covetousness,
wickedness, deceit, lewdness, an evil eye, blasphemy, pride,
foolishness. All these evil things come from within and defile a man" (Mark 7:14-23).

Jesus was disappointed that people were more concerned about what
they put into their bodies than what they put into their minds. What
a Jew ate could make him ceremonially unclean, but impure thoughts
would defile his very heart and soul. Just as the stomach breaks food
down to distribute it throughout the body for nourishment, a similar
process takes place with every thought ingested into the mind. Lingering
thoughts are absorbed into the personality and manifest themselves in
words and deeds. Food eliminated from the body is morally indiffer-
ent, but sinful acts are the waste products of a defiled mind.

In his most joyous epistle, Paul urged the Philippians to make right
thinking a top priority in their daily spiritual regimen. "Finally, brethren,
whatever things are true, whatever things are noble, whatever things
are just, whatever things are pure, whatever things are lovely, whatever things are of good report, if there is any virtue and if there is anything praiseworthy – meditate on these things" (Philippians 4:8). In
corresponding with the troubled Corinthian church, Paul reminded
them that the battle for their souls was waged in the mind: "For though
we walk in the flesh, we do not war according to the flesh. For the
weapons of our warfare are not carnal but mighty in God for pulling
down strongholds, casting down arguments and every high thing that
exalts itself against the knowledge of God, bringing every thought into

captivity to the obedience of Christ" (2 Corinthians 10:3-5). Christian living is unquestionably a product of right thinking.

As a Man Thinketh by James Allen is arguably the best non-inspired book ever written on the power of thought. Allen compared the mind to a garden and its owner to a master gardener. A good character is not the product of chance any more than a beautiful garden could happen by accident. Integrity is a natural result of continued effort in right thinking. Paul also taught that a well-disciplined mind was the key to spiritual transformation: "And do not be conformed to this world, but be transformed by the renewing of your mind, that you may prove what is that good and acceptable and perfect will of God" (Romans 12:2).

The overarching theme of *As a Man Thinketh* is that individuals control the development of their character through controlling their thoughts. At the very moment one chooses his thoughts, he also chooses his destiny. Allen's garden analogy well-illustrates this cause and effect relationship. Just as plants come from seeds, actions grow from thoughts. The challenging part is getting the right seeds into the garden of the mind. Useless seeds find their way there all by themselves, but useful ones must be purposely planted. Good thoughts must be deliberately sown and carefully nurtured to produce the fruit of righteousness. Bad thoughts must be eradicated in the same way one removes weeds to preserve a well-kempt garden. Good thoughts cannot produce bad acts and bad thoughts cannot produce good acts. The law of sowing and reaping is as true in the mental and moral realm as it is in the plant world (Galatians 6:7-8). Holiness, like husbandry, requires planning, effort and diligence.

Reveal the Man

Just as thought affects health and character, it also influences circumstances. Outer conditions are frequently related to an individual's inner state. Consider Joseph who always rose to the top despite his trials. Or consider Daniel who was selected as the Babylonian equivalent of a young Rhodes scholar because of his character and ability. His rise to a position of influence under two world powers was no accident.

All things being equal, a man's circumstances can be altered in direct proportion with the changes he makes in his mental condition. The per-

son who sees himself as a victim of circumstances will be buffeted by
them. An encourager has the spiritual maturity to see circumstances
as opportunities to learn and grow. He knows that his current state of
affairs will shortly pass and give place to new opportunities.

Actually, circumstances have less to do with making a man than
with revealing a man. The thoughts a person secretly fosters in his
heart will manifest themselves when circumstances give them the
chance. Returning to Allen's garden analogy, any train of thought per-
sisted in long enough will, like all seed, bring forth after its kind.
Persistent thoughts solidify into action and crystallize into character.
Circumstances merely bring thought to the surface. Man is limited in
his ability to choose his circumstances directly, but he can do so indi-
rectly by choosing his thoughts. This is why education is a key to ad-
vancement in one's career field, and prayer and meditation are necessary components of spiritual growth.

Circumstances reflect what a person is, not what he wants. Desires
are gratified and prayers are answered when daily thought and activity harmonize with them. That is why James reprimanded the double-
minded man whose prayer requests were disparate with his daily life
(James 1:5-8). Instability is the enemy of success, but the ability to
harness thought opens the door for endless spiritual and secular opportunities. It seems that people are always anxious to change their
circumstances but seldom eager to change themselves. There cannot
be one without the other.

Courageous living occurs when people quit complaining about their
circumstances and start capitalizing on them. Encouragers help others stop blaming and start building. When a courageous person finds
himself in undesirable circumstances, he does not lose heart because
he sees the present moment as an opportunity for new growth (James
1:2). Situations always change, but until they do, Paul provided a motto for encouragers to live by: "Rejoice in the Lord always, again I
will say, rejoice" (Philippians 4:4).

The Pathway to Achievement

Thought affects health, character and circumstance, but when linked
with purpose, it produces human achievement. Too many people drift

aimlessly through life without any plans for the future. Lacking purpose can be as destructive as deliberate wrongdoing. For example, homes taken for granted will not prosper. It takes conscious effort to build a strong marriage and prayerful determination to raise a child to be a decent human being.

Dreams are the cocoon from which reality is born. Christians, above all people, should conceive lofty goals for their lives and strive to achieve them. This relates to the overall goal of going to heaven, but also to more specific areas such as family life and ministry opportunities. Self-control (the ability not to act out every thought) and concentration (the ability to focus thought in a desired direction) are essential to accomplishing worthwhile ends in life. These are character assets lacking in many talented but unsuccessful people.

Courageous people are able to achieve more because they have a healthy way of looking at incomplete attempts. Some people who are quick to call themselves realists will label any aborted effort as failure. Encouragers see the same set of circumstances as a step forward on the pathway to attainment. Every attempt builds strength of character; every effort results in a new starting point the next time. Just as the physically weak become stronger over time by consistent training, they can also become stronger mentally, emotionally and spiritually by exercising right thinking. Encouragers are personal trainers in developing strength of thought.

It is said that vision is the most intimate of all covenants – a pact with one's own heart of the future he will create with God's blessing. Through the power of choice, people make themselves what they are, and only they can alter their course. Even skilled encouragers cannot help someone who refuses to help himself because achievement is the result of combining disciplined thought with extraordinary effort. Progress cannot be made without a willingness to work hard and sacrifice. Sacrifice little and one will accomplish little. Sacrifice much and one can accomplish much. Some thoughts must be relinquished and others must be nurtured. Whatever the goal, the method of achievement is the same.

Just as tall trees come from humble beginnings, all great achievements were once small seedlings of hopeful thought. No one can grow taller or stronger than his most treasured ideas. Great deeds lie dormant in the human mind like plants waiting to be roused from beneath a thin blanket of spring snow. Just as the sun's rays make seeds sprout and open the petals of sleeping flowers, vision has the power to awaken human potential and make achievement possible. Dreams are psychological sunbeams stirring latent hopes from their winter slumber. Character and attainment are the flowering of the soul, the visible blooming of thought into reality.

Just as a houseplant stretches toward a sunlit window, people grow in the direction of their dreams. They are bent by the glow of aspirations that tug at their hearts. But unlike plants, people can generate their own motivational climate. Their lives are shaped by the light and warmth of their most captivating thoughts. Every individual has the ability to produce emotional clouds or sunshine. The single greatest factor in personal development will always be the brightness and boldness with which one dares to dream.

The Power of Thought

Never under estimate the power of thought. Careless, indolent people see achievement and success as a lucky break, but the courageous know differently. One person sees the result, and the other sees the process. Behind every meaningful accomplishment is a trail of blood, sweat and tears known only to men and women of courage who have struggled and triumphed over discouraging, self-defeating thoughts. Those who have never walked that path are oblivious to the trials and sacrifices that must be borne to reach its destination.

A person's life is the result of two things: vision and labor. The greater one's vision and the greater one's labor, the greater one's life. Achievement is not a matter of fate or chance. It is the product of high ideals and heroic endeavor. Those who study hard and struggle long will know success.

Courageous living is a life of high character; of making, using and adapting to circumstances; and of noble achievements accomplished through holy ambition and hard work. It is also a life of calmness. Nothing epitomizes encouragement more than poise under pressure. Composure is the crown of a completed character. Explosive tempers ruin relationships, but those who are patient and poised earn the respect of those who know them. People who have their lives under control by controlling their thoughts experience comparatively greater success, influence and power for good. Encouragement is definitely a frame of mind. Isn't it time you began this new way of thinking?

THINKING LIKE BARNABAS

1. How can thought affect health?

2. Why is the human mind like a garden?

3. How does thought relate to character development?

4. Why can there be no transformation of the life without a renewal of the mind?

5. How does thought impact a person's circumstances in life?

6. Do circumstances make a person or reveal a person?

7. What is the relationship of thought to human achievement?

8. How is an encourager like a personal trainer?

9. How is composure related to thought?

10. Why is the mind the battleground for the soul?

BEHAVING LIKE BARNABAS

1. Break into groups and have each person name something he hopes to accomplish during his lifetime. Have the other group members share positive thoughts that will facilitate the accomplishment of the goal.

2. Ask God to help you adopt an encourager's attitude about life.

3. This week's assignment is to encourage a coworker. Lighten someone's load.

Something that encouraged me last week was ...

Someone I encouraged last week was ...

To become more encouraging this week, I plan to ...

In the past week, I became more or less discouraging in these areas:

- *Insensitivity*   <u>more</u> / less   (*critical, sarcastic, negative*)

- *Intimidation*   more / less   (*bossy, overbearing, threatening*)

- *Ignoring*   more / less   (*preoccupied, aloof, self-centered*)

On a scale of 1 to 10, my use of encouragement skills during the past week was as follows:

- *My mind*   *1 2 3 4 5 6 7 8 9 10*
(*thinking good, pure, positive thoughts*)

- *My eyes*   *1 2 3 4 5 6 7 8 9 10*
(*perceiving the good in every situation*)

- *My ears*   *1 2 3 4 5 6 7 8 9 10*
(*actively and enthusiastically listening*)

- *My lips*   *1 2 3 4 5 6 7 8 9 10*
(*verbally communicating respect and confidence*)

- *My hands*   *1 2 3 4 5 6 7 8 9 10*
(*sensing and acting on opportunities to do good*)

I began each day asking for God's help to become a more encouraging person.
   Yes   *No*

The Eyes of an Encourager

"We are all in the gutter,
but some of us are looking at the stars."

OSCAR WILDE

The human eye is the most valuable organ man has for interacting with the world around him. Eyes are used in nearly everything a person does. The eye does not actually see objects, but it does see the light they give off. Rays of light enter the body through clear tissues and are interpreted as electrical signals that are sent to the brain to produce visual images. Although the eye is quite small, it is powerful enough to see distant objects, such as stars, and tiny objects, such as grains of sand.

An encourager knows his eyes are one of his greatest ministry tools. The eyes can communicate genuine interest and compassion. They are also the means of collecting vital information to be used for encouragement. Anyone wishing to develop the ability to interact more effectively with others should learn how to train the eyes to aid in this process.

Spiritual Blindness

Sight is the most precious of all the human senses and the fear of losing one's eyesight is the most terrifying of all disabilities. Far greater than the loss of physical sight is the danger of spiritual blindness. This point was clearly made by Jesus during an encounter with a group of Pharisees who were upset because He healed a blind man on the Sabbath.

> Now as Jesus passed by, He saw a man who was blind from birth. And His disciples asked Him, saying, "Rabbi, who sinned, this man or his parents, that he was born blind?" Jesus answered, "Neither this man nor his parents sinned, but that the works of God should be revealed in him. I must work the works of Him who sent Me while it is day; the night is coming when no one can work. As long as I am in the world, I am the light of the world." When He had said these things, He spat on the ground and made clay with the saliva; and He anointed the eyes of the blind man with the clay. And He said to him, "Go, wash in the pool of Siloam" (which is translated, Sent). So he went and washed, and came back seeing. ... And Jesus said, "For judgment I have come into this world, that those who do not see may see, and that those who see may be made blind." Then some of the Pharisees who were with Him heard these words, and said to Him, "Are we blind also?" Jesus said to them, "If you were blind, you would have no sin; but now you say, 'We see.' Therefore your sin remains" (John 9:1-7, 39-41).

The eye can see in bright light or dim light, but it cannot see in the absence of light. The same is true of spiritual eyesight. When Jesus said, "I am the light of the world," He revealed that no one can see life clearly without knowing Him. Those who are in spiritual darkness believe they can see, but their image of the world around them is draped in sin. They are like the cartoon character, Mr. McGoo, who confidently strolled through life oblivious to the fact that he courted disaster with every step.

When a person steps down into the waters of baptism, he is entering the pool of Siloam once again. Paul said those who emerge from this watery grave rise to walk in newness of life (Romans 6:4). Entering Christ is like being born all over again. "Therefore, if anyone is in Christ, he is a new creation; old things have passed away; behold, all things have become new" (2 Corinthians 5:17). That newness includes a whole new outlook on life. A Christian can see his spouse, his children, his in-laws, his neighbors, his boss, and even his enemies in a totally new way. He is able to see the purpose and goal of life for the first time. What an experience. It fills the hymn "Amazing Grace!" with new meaning as one sings, "I once was lost, but now am found – Was blind, but now I see."

Although the Great Physician healed the blindness of the physically handicapped man, He could not cure the spiritual infirmity suffered by the Pharisees. The problem was not that He lacked the power to heal them, but that they refused to acknowledge being sick and needing help. They disavowed their blindness and fancied themselves to be leaders of the blind (Matthew 15:14; Romans 2:19). Those who trusted these visually impaired guides to direct them heavenward were certain to end up in a ditch of spiritual disaster.

Spiritual Eye Diseases

Discouraged and discouraging people are convinced that their view of the world is true. Their inability to see life properly is evidence of spiritual eye disease. Just as cataracts cloud the vision and interfere with a person's daily activities, sin can obscure the ability to see other people and life's opportunities in a healthful way.

Defects of the eyes such as myopia (nearsightedness) or hyperopia (farsightedness) are debilitating without proper treatment. Spiritual myopia is shortsightedness that occurs when a person has no compelling vision of the future to guide his actions today. Spiritual hyperopia ensues when a person is unable to see good in his present circumstances and closest relationships, but imagines things are better than they really are for everyone else. Fortunately, this grass-always-looks-greener-on-the-other-side-of-the-fence syndrome is correctable with Jesus' help.

Learning to Focus

The eye's ability to focus is one of its most amazing features. It can quickly adjust between objects that are near and far and even direct its attention to a given object when the head is moving. Learning to focus is one of the key skills needed by good encouragers.

Many kinds of stimuli vie for people's attention, but individuals are free to choose what they will concentrate upon. Consider a student in a typical classroom. Will he choose to listen to the lecture, converse with his classmate, doodle, pass notes, or daydream about his plans for the afternoon? Sights and sounds in and around the classroom compete for the student's attention, yet he will focus primarily on one.

Now narrow the scope of possibilities to that which is good and bad. People will generally feature one and forget the other. Discouragers unconsciously focus on the negative, while encouragers consciously focus on the positive. The difference is dramatic. What a person chooses to accentuate will impact his or her ability to relate effectively. The ability to see good in people and situations is the cornerstone of encouragement. It is a skill that does not appear accidentally or by magic. It takes training.

Why are most people unskilled at noticing the good around them? It is because modern culture is mistake-oriented. The media makes its living on publicizing what is worst in people and society. Verbal attacks are the stock and trade of political campaigns. More than half the couples pledging undying love to each other develop tunnel vision of the heart, a malady rendering them incapable of seeing any redeeming quality in their mate. Supervisors scold, coaches castigate, parents pester, and teachers tongue lash. A person growing up in America will have no lack of exposure to nitpicking and faultfinding.

Discouragement is a communicable disease more infectious than the flu. Negativity is an airborne ailment transmitted from person to person through words, looks and casual social contact. Criticism spreads from one discouraging relationship to another until it reaches epidemic proportions. The outbreak can engulf families, businesses, schools, churches and entire communities. Only encouragement can halt the advance of this plague. It takes real effort to cultivate the habit of focusing on the good, perhaps because the good is not always readily visible. Some people are rough, unpolished diamonds, and it takes a perceptive person to bring out their shine.

Encouragers are in the reclamation business. Their job is to salvage sunken self-esteem. Like divers who retrieve lost treasure from submerged ships, so encouragers strive to reclaim wrecked confidence and foundering hope. People's best qualities often lurk beneath the surface. Riches resting at the bottom of the sea are of no benefit unless they can be raised. Similarly, the gifts and talents of discouraged people must be brought to the surface if they are to be enjoyed.

Christians must recognize that they are stewards of their relationships and that people have been placed in their circle of influence to receive encouragement. To fulfill that role, it is necessary for saints to reorient their thinking and transform their values. It all begins with resigning as human fault inspectors and resolving to accentuate the positive.

Seeing the Glory in the Ordinary

It is crucial for would-be encouragers to see the glory of the ordinary. That does not mean mediocrity is to be celebrated as virtuous. It does mean that when an ordinary person is striving to rise above his current level of attainment, it is something worthy of commendation. Anybody can applaud the outstanding athlete or artist, but is perfection all that is worthy of praise? When average people experience personal growth, it is wrong to denigrate their accomplishments through comparisons with others. What matters is that they have shattered the limiting barrier of their past performance and reached new levels of achievement. That is something to brag about.

We also have a tendency to withhold encouragement in a deserving area of a person's life because of a less noble facet in a different area. Recognizing one trait does not mean condoning all. Skillful encouragers can see the good in any individual. Will Rogers once said that he never met a man he did not like. Most people would admit that they have met individuals they did not care for, but that misses Rogers' point. He did not mean that he liked every quality of every person he ever knew. Rather, he was saying that he never met someone in whom there was not something to like. When others would despair, Rogers would set out in discovery. There are times when finding the good may seem challenging, but it can be done.

When Paul found it necessary to rebuke a church or an individual, he would begin by complimenting them. He wanted to be sure they knew he did not reject them as persons. Proportionality is an important encouragement principle. Words of admonition and correction have no power unless there is a positive relationship behind them.

When parents continuously scold their children, they will eventually tune them out. Habitual naggers are impossible to please, so why bother trying? Wise parents look for every opportunity to praise. When correction is absolutely necessary, children will not doubt that they are loved. A strong family bond makes them want to please their parents. Because criticism is so infrequent, they really listen when Mom or Dad speak out.

Paul was talking about this when he said, "fathers, do not provoke your children to wrath, but bring them up in the training and admonition of the Lord" (Ephesians 6:4). Disproportionate criticism is ineffective, regardless of the accuracy of the statement or the good intention behind it. All that it does is alienate others and entrench them in their unhealthful behavior.

Look Through Caring Eyes

Although there is a time and place for caring intervention between Christians, no one has the right or duty to mote hunt (Matthew 7:1-5). Christians are to look at others through caring eyes. Traits first perceived as negative may be positive when examined in the light of love. Without being naive, encouragers should make it a habit to put the best possible construction on any situation. The discourager sees John as stubborn, but the encourager considers him persistent and determined. The critic sees Jane as bossy, but the consoler sees her as an assertive person who gets results. The faultfinder says Bob talks too much, but the positive person says he is outgoing and friendly, a real people person.

A discourager is like a doctor with a poor bedside manner. Rather than seeing a patient, he sees a diagnosis or a source of income. Impersonal physicians can heal sick bodies, but they fail miserably in treating the fear, anxiety and loneliness that ails their clientele. In contrast, a good doctor sees each patient as a friend and treats the whole person. Encouragers see people while complainers only see problems.

Becoming an encourager is like putting on a pair of glasses for the first time. Everything looks more beautiful when seen in clear focus. A near-sighted child who is fitted with corrective lenses is thrilled to see leaves on the trees and fish in the stream. Encouragement is corrective lenses for the soul. It is amazing what one can see with a loving focus.

A skilled encourager can always see something to affirm in others. Do they have a good attitude? Do they take pride in their appearance? Do they possess a special talent or ability? If they cannot be praised for completed actions, can they be congratulated for their attempts? Encouragers notice effort and progress, not just perfect performance. They can see what people are capable of and how things can be with a little encouragement to sustain their faltering footsteps.

Unrealistic Standards

Unrealistic standards can be a formidable barrier to personal growth. The woman who says, "I won't be happy until I weigh 100 pounds" may be setting herself up for failure and discouragement. The man who says, "I won't be satisfied until I complete my first marathon" may de-prive himself of the pride he should feel for running a 10k. In most cases, it is a big mistake to decide, "I won't be happy until … ." Ignoring or discounting small achievements can be emotionally destructive.

Just as children must walk before they can run, so it is with all mean-ingful accomplishments. Encouragers are like proud parents who glee-fully celebrate their child's first steps. It is difficult to imagine a par-ent shrugging at that glorious moment and saying, "When you win the Boston Marathon, then I will be impressed." There are many small steps to be enjoyed along the pathway of life. To overlook the signif-icance of these milestones is to be deprived of immeasurable joy. Success is much more of a journey than a destination. Perceiving and praising effort will provide a significant push in the right direction at a time when it is sorely needed. Never minimize small steps forward. It is not the size of the stride but the direction that counts.

The Joy in Being an Encourager

Nothing is more fun than encouraging others. It is exhilarating to see people radiate with newfound confidence. Encouragers are tal-ent scouts who help people discover their inherent worth and hidden ability. At church services, Christians sing "Just As I Am!" and exult in God's capacity to love imperfect people. Encouragers please God when they value people as they are but strive to help them reach their potential.

It is sad but true that many close relationships tend to be discouraging. When Job was suffering intense emotional and physical pain, he was visited by four friends who were miserable comforters (Job16:2, 15-20). Their coming added to his burden rather than lightening his load. Christians must not allow their influence to be negative or even neutral. Learn to perceive the positive in any situation. As Paul said, "Rejoice always, pray without ceasing, in everything give thanks; for this is the will of God in Christ Jesus for you" (1 Thessalonians 5:16-18).

THINKING LIKE BARNABAS

1. Why is the eye an encourager's most valuable ministry tool?

2. How are discouragers similar to Mr. McGoo?

3. Why is baptism like washing in the Pool of Siloam?

4. Discuss discouragement being spiritual farsightedness. Nearsightedness.

5. Does affirming the glory of the ordinary promote mediocrity?

6. What is the law of proportionality as it relates to encouragement?

7. How is a discouraging person like a doctor with a poor bedside manner?

8. How is encouragement like corrective lenses for the soul?

9. Why is it harmful to discount small steps toward the completion of a goal?

10. How are encouragers like talent scouts?

BEHAVING LIKE BARNABAS

1. Break into groups and distribute poster board and magic markers for making a spiritual eye chart. Accompany each letter with a

word describing something an encouraging person would look for in a person or situation.

2. Pray for more perceptive and caring eyes as ministers of encouragement.

3. This week's assignment is to encourage your closest neighbor. Don't put it off.

Something that encouraged me last week was ...

Someone I encouraged last week was ...

To become more encouraging this week, I plan to ...

In the past week, I became more or less discouraging in these areas:

- *Insensitivity*   *more / less*   (*critical, sarcastic, negative*)

- *Intimidation*   *more / less*   (*bossy, overbearing, threatening*)

- *Ignoring*   *more / less*   (*preoccupied, aloof, self-centered*)

On a scale of 1 to 10, my use of encouragement skills during the past week was as follows:

- My *mind*   *1 2 3 4 5 6 7 8 9 10*
  (*thinking good, pure, positive thoughts*)

- My *eyes*   *1 2 3 4 5 6 7 8 9 10*
  (*perceiving the good in every situation*)

- My *ears*   *1 2 3 4 5 6 7 8 9 10*
  (*actively and enthusiastically listening*)

- My *lips*   *1 2 3 4 5 6 7 8 9 10*
  (*verbally communicating respect and confidence*)

- My *hands*   *1 2 3 4 5 6 7 8 9 10*
  (*sensing and acting on opportunities to do good*)

I began each day asking for God's help to become a more encouraging person.
   Yes   *No*

The Ears of an Encourager

"Courage is what it takes to stand up and speak; courage is also what it takes to sit down and listen."

SIR WINSTON CHURCHILL

Of all the skills needed by an encourager, listening is arguably the most essential. It is also the most difficult. That is because listening is more a matter of the heart and mind than of the ears. Mastering the art of communication requires not only hearing, but also understanding and caring.

Listening Involves Determination

The human will also plays a crucial role in the communication process. Encouragers must resolve to develop their listening skills with the same commitment needed for success in other fields of endeavor. Success in athletics, academics or the arts does not happen by chance. The exceptional performance of overachievers is the end result of a process of hard work, and becoming a good listener is one of the hardest things a person will ever do. Cultivating the ability to encourage through listening will require uncommon determination.

Listening appears to be easy, but looks can be deceiving. If listening is so simple, why are there so few good listeners? What percentage of people with whom you converse are proficient in this skill? How accomplished are you at listening? Communication is not as effortless as it may seem at first. As stated earlier, competency requires commitment.

Trying to communicate can be one of the most discouraging things a person does. How does a poor listener make you feel? An employee shares a new idea with his boss and notices that he keeps looking at his watch. A woman tries to tell her husband about her day, but he never stops changing channels on the television. A parent attempts to have a heart-to-heart talk with a teenager who keeps staring into space. These are just a few of the ways that people hurt and discourage each other every day. Although no harm is intended, the pain is real.

The level of communication that takes place in most conversations is superficial to say the least. Most people enjoy talking much more than listening. Frequently, they will simply take turns speaking without anyone paying serious attention to the other's message. Conversation is typically not dialogue but two concurrent and competing monologues.

The appearance of receptivity can often be deceptive. Being silent is not the same as listening. If, rather than striving to comprehend, a person pauses only to think of what to say next, he has failed in his responsibility.

Still, no one should ever despair over his ability to excel as a listener. Encouragers do not have to be perfect to be proficient. Being a good communicator is within the grasp of everyone. Desire is the difference between becoming an encouraging listener or becoming entrenched in discouraging, self-defeating communication habits. Anyone who wants to improve as a listener can do so with God's help (Philippians 4:13).

Listening Is Loving

The core problem in failed communication is selfishness. Self-interest can manifest itself in numerous ways during a conversation. It dominates the theme and direction of discussions. It is visible in a listener's countenance and body language. Indifference can be heard in the lack of enthusiasm in one's tone of voice. Insensitivity to the feelings of others can hinder communication and hurt future relations with that person.

If selfishness is the cause of unsuccessful communication, then caring is the cure. Listening is loving. Agape love is much more than a warm feeling. It is graciously acting in the best interest of others out of genuine concern for their well-being and happiness. In some instances, it is possible to have a greater impact on others by how one listens rather than what one says. The way a person listens can rapidly and dramatically change the way others feel about him.

Nothing is more encouraging than a good listener, because few things affect a person's self-concept more than the way others react to his words. Listening shows the value a hearer places on the speaker, and Christians should make it their aim to regard each person as important. Everyone wants to feel heard, understood and respected. When these needs go unfulfilled, the effect on the speaker's ego can be devastating although the problem rests mainly with the other person.

The rewards of good listening are abundant. It cements relationships, instills self-confidence, and facilitates the accomplishment of worthwhile aims. When it comes to relationships, goodwill is much like money in the bank. When a person feels loved and valued, it is possible to draw on the strength of that bond. If a person feels misunderstood or taken for granted, the account is overdrawn.

A Christian Characteristic

Good listening is more than a useful tool. It is a Christian characteristic. If children of God are to become more like their Father in heaven, they must raise the level of their listening skills. When the Israelites were suffering as slaves in Egypt, God spoke to Moses at the burning bush and told him, "I have surely seen the oppression of My people who are in Egypt, and have heard their cry because of their taskmasters, for I know their sorrows" (Exodus 3:7).

When Solomon prayed to God during the dedication of the newly constructed temple, the Lord responded, "I have heard your prayer and your supplication that you have made before Me; I have consecrated this house which you have built to put My name there forever, and My eyes and My heart will be there perpetually" (1 Kings 9:3).

After King Hezekiah was stricken with a terminal illness, he turned his face toward the wall and poured out his soul in prayer to God. The

Lord delivered His reply through the prophet Isaiah saying, "Return and tell Hezekiah the leader of My people, 'Thus says the Lord, the God of David your father: I have heard your prayer, I have seen your tears; surely I will heal you. On the third day you shall go up to the house of the Lord'" (2 Kings 20:5). In times of suffering or times of joy, God listens closely to His people. His example is both inspiring and challenging.

Jesus, Our Example

Jesus modeled impressive listening skills. Many people who had grown accustomed to being ignored found a receptive listener in Him. When Jesus was passing through Jericho, a blind man sat by the side of the road desperately pleading for assistance. Despite the volume of his entreaties, the throng accompanying Jesus filtered out his cries until they were barely heard. Even those who heard his voice did not hear his pain. "Jesus, Son of David, have mercy on me" (Mark 10:47). While some in the crowd warned Bartimaeus to be quiet, Jesus stopped what He was doing, approached him, and gave him His full attention. It was an impressive moment in the life of the Messiah. Never was His divinity more on display than when He took the time to listen, really listen, to ordinary people He encountered each day.

In addition to modeling good listening, Jesus constantly taught His disciples the value of cultivating advanced listening skills. When Jesus told a parable, He frequently closed with a statement emphasizing that it would take more than passing interest to comprehend His words: "He who has ears to hear, let him hear" (Matthew 13:9; Deuteronomy 29:4; Ezekiel 12:2). Listening must involve the heart as well as the head. It is common for a person to think he understands a speaker's message when he has completely missed the point. Jesus was calling His followers to develop a deeper level of hearing. Whether attending to the words of God or the words of a grandchild, Christians benefit from adopting a more thoughtful and determined style of listening.

Those who were fortunate enough to associate with Jesus during His earthly ministry learned these communication principles firsthand. Each day, as they watched Him interact with others, they took mental notes about how to improve their relational skills. Few people spent

as much time with Jesus as His own family. Although
ers did not believe on Him at first, they cast away any l
after His resurrection. After they came to faith and grew
of leadership in the church, they must have reflected on t
time they spent with Him. It is no wonder that James, in
chapter of his letter addressing the practical implications of Christianity,
should choose to talk about listening.

James' Advice About Listening

"So then, my beloved brethren, let every man be swift to hear, slow
to speak, slow to wrath; for the wrath of man does not produce the
righteousness of God" (James 1:19-20). These words refer primarily to
man's relationship with God, but who could question whether these
concepts would also help people relate more effectively with those created in the image of God? These three simple steps can revolutionize
the existing bond between human beings.

James advised his readers to act in a way that is out of character
with their natural tendencies. It is far more common for men and
women to be slow to hear, quick to speak, and to explode in anger
over the most trivial things. Although this kind of behavior is clearly counter-productive, it is the most typical pattern of human inter-
action. James is stating with conviction that it does not have to be
that way. Husbands and wives are not destined to go on hurting each
other. Parents and children are not bound to break each other's hearts.
Neighbors are not fated to feud with one another. Rather than being
doomed to inflict pain on others, Christians can choose to impart
help, hope and healing. But how?

• *"Be swift to hear."* All healthy relationships begin with listening. When couples or coworkers stop listening, it generally marks
the beginning of the end. Slowly but surely, the relationship will dis-
integrate without the cement of communication. Respectful listening
is the adhesive that hold families, friends, churches and successful businesses together. Careless listening is a relational solvent that eats away
at the most precious ties of life.

Being "swift" or "quick" (NIV) to hear suggests an underlying attitude
that is the foundation of successful communication. The word "quick"

rom the Greek *"tachus,"* and occurs only once in the New Testament. It typically refers to someone who is fleet of foot, but here it speaks of a state of mind. Being swift or speedy to hear refers to a ready disposition to listen.

Encouragers should mentally prepare themselves to listen with the intensity of a baseball player set to field any ball that comes his way. Before a fielder can do anything else, he must catch the ball. Before a listener can speak, he must catch the meaning of the person addressing him. Failure to pick up on the speaker's message results in a communication "error." If a person would like to improve his influence by a quantum leap, he should attempt to understand the viewpoint and feelings of others before talking himself.

• *"Slow to speak"* means a Christian should exercise self-control when engaged in oral communication. It is not honorable or advisable to say anything that comes to mind. One should reserve his comments until he is sure he knows what he is talking about. When he does speak, he should consider how his words may be perceived by the other person to avoid misunderstanding. Communication involves result as well as intent.

• *"Slow to wrath"* underscores the value of patience in dialogue. Once a person becomes angry, communication suffers. There is a valid place for righteous indignation in the life of a Christian, but he must not become upset too easily. When a person gets angry, he quits listening, and his words and manner tend to alienate others. Estrangement can often be traced back to a thoughtless moment of rage. Hostility may result more from faulty communication patterns than from issues of real importance.

Learning to listen is the single greatest thing you can do to become a more encouraging person. Nothing else will help you relate more effectively. Nothing else will have a greater impact on shaping the way others think about you. Consistent, compassionate, committed listening is the encouragement skill most needed and most lacking in people's lives. Make up your mind to become an exceptional listener and start enjoying the benefits of better relationships today.

An Anatomy Lesson for Encouraging Listeners

• *Listen with muscle.* Roll up your sleeves and get ready to invest yourself wholly in the conversation. It is hard to listen actively and will require great inner strength to stay on track. Enter conversations with a commitment to give the other person your all.

• *Listen with your ears.* The unimpeded transmission of audio signals is the most rudimentary part of receiving another person's message. Noisy distractions such as radio and television should be eliminated. Find a quiet spot where you can pick up on nuances of communication that might be missed in a crowded room.

• *Listen with your eyes.* Mastering nonverbal communication is essential for people who want to become encouraging listeners. Look closely at the other person's body language to get a more accurate interpretation of his verbal message. Remember that he is watching you too. Let your eyes show alertness and interest. Avoid staring off into space, or he may get the feeling you are focused on your thoughts rather than his message. Refrain from extreme gestures such as rolling your eyes. The speaker will interpret it to mean shock or disagreement and will talk less openly.

• *Listen with your lips.* Use small talk or reassuring words to set people at ease when they come to speak with you. Let the other person do most of the talking but don't go overboard with silence. Ask brief questions to let people know you want them to continue, or restate what you heard to help them clarify their message. Do not change subjects unless you are sure the speaker is ready. Never quarrel, and restrict, delay and be innovative with criticism.

• *Listen with your head.* In addition to the responsibility borne by each of its members, the head as a unit may also facilitate better communication. Leaning the head slightly forward or stretching the neck toward the speaker says, "You have my attention." If the head is bowed forward or leaned back, it suggests the hearer, although contemplative, is consumed with his own thoughts. Slowly nodding the head is an affirming action. This gentle back and forth motion grants the speaker your approval to keep talking.

• *Listen with your body.* The trunk of a person's body is a full partner in the communication process. Although its language is more discreet, it still sends an important message. Encouraging listeners should avoid slouching that might suggest disinterest. By sitting erect and occasionally leaning forward, the listener can let the speaker know he is enthusiastically attentive.

• **Listen with your hands.** Put down pencils and small objects you may be tempted to fidget with. Reach out your hand to make a warm human connection with the speaker. When it is appropriate, a pat on the back or a quick embrace is a powerful way to let the other person know he is safe and can speak freely in your presence.

• **Listen with your mind.** Good listeners know that words cannot transfer a speaker's exact thought into the mind of a hearer. Miscommunication is always a possibility, so it is important for the listener to check and double check what he thinks he has heard. It is common for faxes to be garbled in transmission or lost and never received. Verbal messages can also become confused in transit so do not take understanding for granted.

• **Listen with your feet.** Stand up and greet people who want to speak to you. Move closer without crowding to show more interest. When the conversation is winding down, patiently walk with them as they leave. Backing up or walking away while listening is rude under most circumstances. Don't give people the idea that you are hurried or that they are not important to you.

• **Listen with your heart.** The most important tool in listening is the human heart. Listen empathetically to what a speaker is saying. As much as possible, set aside your own concerns and agenda and listen unselfishly and compassionately. Apply the Golden Rule by being the kind of listener you would want if you were doing the talking. Try to imagine yourself in the other person's situation. Hold your temper and avoid passing judgment until you are certain you have all the facts. Let a genuine concern for the well-being of the speaker guide your actions.

THINKING LIKE BARNABAS

1. Why is listening the most difficult encouragement skill to master?

2. How does selfishness interfere with listening?

3. Why is listening synonymous with loving?

4. What are some of the rewards of good listening?

5. What kind of listener was Jesus?

6. What does it mean to be "quick to hear"?

7. Why is it important for encouragers to be "slow to speak"?

8. How does wrath interfere with the communication process?

9. What does it mean to say that "communication is result as well as intent"?

10. How dangerous is a careless listener?

BEHAVING LIKE BARNABAS

1. Have everyone pair off and discuss their most recent vacations. Every time someone uses the personal pronoun "I," "me" or "my" have him sit down. The one left standing will start up a new conversation once someone else's partner is seated. See how difficult it is to talk about others rather than self.

2. Get a partner and take turns practicing encouraging listening skills. Use favorite hobbies as the topic of discussion. Switch roles after 3 minutes.

3. Ask for God's help to become a more encouraging listener.

4. This week's assignment is to encourage a deacon in your church. Make him glow.

Something that encouraged me last week was ...

Someone I encouraged last week was ...

To become more encouraging this week, I plan to ...

In the past week, I became more or less discouraging in these areas:

- Insensitivity   more / less   (critical, sarcastic, negative)

- Intimidation   more / less   (bossy, overbearing, threatening)

- Ignoring   more / less   (preoccupied, aloof, self-centered)

On a scale of 1 to 10, my use of encouragement skills during the past week was as follows:

- My mind   1 2 3 4 5 6 7 8 9 10
(thinking good, pure, positive thoughts)

- My eyes   1 2 3 4 5 6 7 8 9 10
(perceiving the good in every situation)

- My ears   1 2 3 4 5 6 7 8 9 10
(actively and enthusiastically listening)

- My lips   1 2 3 4 5 6 7 8 9 10
(verbally communicating respect and confidence)

- My hands   1 2 3 4 5 6 7 8 9 10
(sensing and acting on opportunities to do good)

I began each day asking for God's help to become a more encouraging person.
   Yes   No

The Lips of an Encourager

"Flatter me, and I may not believe you. Criticize me, and I may not like you. Ignore me, and I may not forgive you. Encourage me, and I may not forget you."

WILLIAM ARTHUR WARD

Good communication is vitally important if the church is to fulfill its mission as a haven of encouragement in a disheartening world. The church is more than buildings, professional ministers, and exciting programs. The church is people – people of faith energizing one another through fellowship. If a church is to justify its existence, its worthiness of devotion, and its right to continue and grow, then it must know its purpose. The church is not a business enterprise, and it is much more than a self-perpetuating bureaucracy. First and foremost, it is relationship.

Christianity is about knowing Christ more intimately (Philippians 3:8-11), but it also involves getting to know and care about other people. Peter exhorted his readers, "Since you have purified your souls in obeying the truth through the Spirit in sincere love of the brethren, love one another fervently with a pure heart" (1 Peter 1:22). Fellowship in the church is God's unique and indispensable means of providing His followers with spiritual encouragement. Whenever Christians assemble, God's purpose in bringing them together is to increase their love for each other.

The ministry of encouragement is the privilege and responsibility of every faithful Christian. Saints are obligated to "consider one another in order to stir up love and good works" (Hebrews 10:24). When a brother in Christ experiences a difficulty that weakens his commitment to Christ, it is a sacred duty to intervene compassionately rather than look the other way (3:12-13). The community of faith is a fellowship where people informally and spontaneously motivate each other to walk more closely with the Lord. That is why the galvanizing core of the church is relationship. Through deeper ties with one another, saints cultivate deeper ties with Christ.

The Power of Words

Relationship is the heart of Christianity, and communication is the heart of relationship. If the church were a building, communication would be the plumbing. When pipes get clogged, trouble is not far behind. The free flow of encouraging words is as essential to spiritual life as water is to physical life. Yet good water must be pure – not rusty, bitter or contaminated.

> But no man can tame the tongue. It is an unruly evil, full of deadly poison. With it we bless our God and Father, and with it we curse men, who have been made in the similitude of God. Out of the same mouth proceed blessing and cursing. My brethren, these things ought not to be so. Does a spring send forth fresh water and bitter from the same opening? Can a fig tree, my brethren, bear olives, or a grapevine bear figs? Thus no spring can yield both salt water and fresh (James 3:8-12).

James declared the words of a Christian should be as pure and refreshing to the hearer as a cool drink of spring water. Even when rebuke is necessary, it is possible to speak the truth with such obvious love that words of admonition have the healing effect of the therapeutic waters of a hot spring.

Solomon wrote, "Pleasant words are like a honeycomb, Sweetness to the soul and health to the bones" (Proverbs 16:24). Israel's most noted sage revealed the difference between health and sickness can sometimes be accounted for by the pleasantness or unpleasantness of spoken words. Does language really possess such power? Solomon certainly believed so, as did the Holy Spirit who guided this prolific writer. Listen to the wisdom of this master encourager: "Anxiety in the heart of man causes depression, But a good word makes it glad" (Proverbs 12:25). "A wholesome tongue is a tree of life, But perverseness in it breaks the spirit" (15:4). "Death and life are in the power of the tongue" (18:21).

From these verses we learn that a good word can be the difference between depression and gladness. It can break the human spirit or build strong self-esteem. For someone who is deeply discouraged, it can actually be the difference between life and death. The conclusion is that encouraging words are the centerpiece of healthy human relationships, or as Solomon put it, "A word fitly spoken is like apples of gold In settings of silver" (Proverbs 25:11).

James also affirmed the life-changing power of words:

> Indeed, we put bits in horses' mouths that they may obey us, and we turn their whole body. Look also at ships: although they are so large and are driven by fierce winds, they are turned by a very small rudder wherever the pilot desires. Even so the tongue is a little member and boasts great things. See how great a forest a little fire kindles. And the tongue is a fire, a world of iniquity. The tongue is so set among our members that it defiles the whole body, and sets on fire the course of nature; and it is set on fire by hell (James 3:3-6).

Small things can impact their environment in big ways. A tiny bit in a horse's mouth can control the direction and speed of one of the largest and strongest animals on earth. Massive seagoing vessels can navigate rough seas and transport large quantities of cargo from continent to continent thanks to a relatively small steering device.

What could be smaller than a spark, yet it can kindle a forest fire that will engulf thousands of acres of timberland. Most forest fires are not started by arsonists but by negligent campers and travelers. Similarly, a careless word can be intensely painful and destructive. Once it begins its work, no one can foresee where its carnage will end. Besides devastating families and friendships, it can jeopardize the very soul of the

speaker. Thoughtless or malicious speech can put a person on a colli-
sion course with hell. Christians must never underestimate the ability of their words to wound and destroy or to inspire and heal.

Praise is one of the most powerful forms of encouragement known
to man. People everywhere are hungering for respect and recognition.
They yearn for the soul food of encouragement.

Discouraged people are like houseplants that need nurturing to survive. If neglected, a plant's leaves begin to wither and turn brown. If
ignored, people seem to wilt as their heads lower and their shoulders
droop. Give a forgotten plant a little water and sunshine and it has an
amazing capacity to revive. Give a depressed person a little praise and,
in many cases, he will rejuvenate before your eyes. Encouragers are
gardeners of the soul, and words are the tools of their trade.

Using Your Words Wisely

• *Think Carefully.* Here are some suggestions for becoming more
encouraging in your speech. First, think twice before speaking. Average
people are more likely to be negative than positive in what they say.
In the beginning, it takes a concerted effort to change the habit of being predominantly critical, so "Bite your tongue." It makes no difference if the words were well-intended. Millions of people unwittingly
devastate their friends and family members on a daily basis. Results
are what count, so keep that tongue under control until weighing the
impact words will have on the other person. Consider how they might
hear it, not just how it was intended.

• *Compliment Credibly.* Make sure that compliments are credible. Insincere words have about the same value as Confederate cur-
rency. People have a way of sensing whether praise is genuine or pho-
ny. Encouraging words must surpass the pleasantries of pretentious
maitre d's whose words were bought and paid for with the meal. The
words of an encourager do not have to be momentous, but they must
be heartfelt. If you do not believe it, do not say it. Hollow words can
discourage as much as hurtful words.

• *Praise Creatively.* In some situations, it is difficult to think of
something positive to say, but the problem is usually with the speaker's standards rather than the other person's performance. Do not with-

hold praise for anything less than perfection. A competent perform-ance by someone doing his best is more deserving of accolades than the effortless performance of a more gifted person. Take notice of progress as well as accomplishment. Express faith in a person's ability to succeed. Let him know that you believe in him and give him a rep-utation and self-image to live up to. Carefully select words that can turn cold impersonal compliments into motivational expressions of enthusiastic confidence.

• *Speak Specifically.* Experienced encouragers know the importance of praising with precision. When a preacher stands at the rear of the auditorium after finishing his sermon, the congregation smiles, shakes his hand, and says, "Good lesson." The possible interpretations of those words are far ranging, but most ministers will translate them to mean "Pretty average." Then someone pauses at the door, looks the preach-er in the eye, and says, "I was really moved this morning when you made the point about ... ." You would think that the heavens had opened and he was hearing the "Hallelujah Chorus" led by Michael himself. What was the difference but specificity? When a husband says, "Honey, you look nice today," she may shrug it off, but if he says, "Darling, you look terrific in that blue dress!" she will glow.

• *Inspire Indelibly.* Writing is a highly effective method of en-couragement. This advice is not to denigrate the spoken word, but there is something special about words of praise written on paper. Cards and letters express love because of the forethought and effort they require. There is also the advantage of being able to preserve and sa-vor written words. If spoken over the phone, the same message would have a fleeting influence, but when written, it can be mounted on the refrigerator, pressed in a book, or tucked away in a special drawer where it can be pulled out and read again and again. Write notes at special times such as holidays and birthdays, but "just thinking of you" notes can be the most treasured of all.

Be an Encourager Now

The letter to the Hebrews was written to provide Jewish Christians with courage to cling to their faith. The writer chose a stirring ath-letic analogy to connect with his readers on an emotional level.

Therefore we also, since we are surrounded by so great a
cloud of witnesses, let us lay aside every weight, and the sin
which so easily ensnares us, and let us run with endurance
the race that is set before us, looking unto Jesus, the author
and finisher of our faith, who for the joy that was set before
Him endured the cross, despising the shame, and has sat
down at the right hand of the throne of God. For consider Him who endured such hostility from sinners against
Himself, lest you become weary and discouraged in your
souls (Hebrews 12:1-3).

This image of righteous men and women from the past urging saints
to stay the course is thrilling. Still, too many people think it is necessary to be deceased to enter heaven's cheering section. To the contrary,
Christians can take their place on the encouragement team at this very
moment. It is hard to overestimate the difference encouragement can
make in the performance of an exhausted athlete or a dispirited saint.

All Christians are bound to experience spiritual fatigue and cramps
at some point. What should be said as they hobble and limp along?
It is sad to see someone drop out of a race, but especially when the
crowd is cheering madly and the finish line is in sight. Just as it is
unimaginable for a coach to heckle a weary runner as he struggles
toward the tape, so Christians must never speak a word that might add
to the burden of a discouraged brother. As for the Hebrew writer, what
was his message to potential apostates? "But, beloved, we are confident of better things concerning you, yes, things that accompany
salvation" (Hebrews 6:9).

James declared that words are a good indicator of a person's spiritual status (James 1:26). Christians must never go through a day, let alone
a lifetime, oblivious to the impact of their words on their brethren and
neighbors. Paul also made an impassioned plea for developing the skill
of encouraging through words.

Let no corrupt word proceed out of your mouth, but what
is good for necessary edification, that it may impart grace
to the hearers. And do not grieve the Holy Spirit of God,
by whom you were sealed for the day of redemption. Let all

bitterness, wrath, anger, clamor, and evil speaking be put away from you, with all malice. And be kind to one another, tenderhearted, forgiving one another, even as God in Christ forgave you (Ephesians 4:29-32).

Bitter, angry words born of malice have no right to be aired. There is no first amendment in God's kingdom guaranteeing this kind of free speech. Paul said "Let no corrupt word proceed out of your mouth." Some things do not need to be said. Let God's Spirit be spared the unnecessary grief of hearing evil words that are destined to devastate and discourage those He has worked so hard to redeem.

What is the standard for Christian speech? It is summed up in three simple questions:

(1) Is what I am saying true both in fact and impression?

(2) Is what I am saying helpful to the listener? To the person about whom I speak?

(3) Is what I am saying tempered by kindness and consideration for other's feelings?

How to Discourage the Flow of Communication

• *Interrupt.* When a listener interrupts, it indicates that he made up his mind before hearing all the facts. Jumping to conclusions short circuits healthy communication. Unconsciously, the interrupter is saying "I am smarter than you, and what I have to say is more important than what you are saying." Unless the building is on fire, don't interrupt.

• *Criticize.* Most critics justify their words on the basis of their intentions. They classify their comments as constructive and believe they should be gratefully welcomed by the recipient. The problem is that most criticism only masquerades as constructive. Rather than being helpful, it is hurtful. The vast majority of criticism is unjust, uncaring and untimely. Think twice before you criticize.

• *Advise.* When someone tells you about a problem, don't try to solve it unless he asks you to. He is probably using you as a sounding board to think things through. He may simply want someone to know what he is going through. Unsolicited advice may be interpreted by the recipient as implying his incompetence or lack of intelligence. Give others your support but don't offer solutions unless they are requested.

• **Embarrass.** There is no excuse for publicly ridiculing another person. Thoughtless parents belittle their children in front of relatives and friends. Sadistic spouses take devilish delight in mortifying their mates in social settings. Tyrannical managers think nothing of berating underlings within earshot of co-workers. Lectures and reproof are best reserved for private. Public derision creates bitter resentment that will not soon be forgotten. Upholding the dignity of subordinates creates lasting good will.

• **Condescend.** People in positions of responsibility must pay attention to what they say and how they say it. It is easy to slip into an authoritarian posture or tone that the hearer feels is demeaning. No one likes being talked down to. Besides wounding someone's pride, condescension creates an "us" and "them" mentality that blocks communication and cooperation. Speak to others as equals who merely occupy a different role. That respect will be both appreciated and reciprocated.

• **Blame.** It is far better to work on solutions than to assign blame. Strategizing means looking forward while criticizing requires looking backward. Energy is better devoted to solving problems than assaulting personalities. There are compelling reasons to identify and censure individuals guilty of serious wrongdoing, but honest mistakes are better overlooked in many instances.

• **Overreact.** Put things into perspective before you go ballistic next time. Making a mountain out of a molehill will alienate others and cause them to discount your opinion in the future. Blowing up demonstrates a lack of character and self-control that lowers others' esteem for you.

• **Distort.** In situations where you hold strong opinions and allegiances, it is easy to color the facts to fit your case. Strive for complete honesty and impartiality in communication, especially when dealing with those of competing viewpoints. Represent the facts of the case and the position of those who differ from you as accurately and graciously as possible. Your fair treatment will garner goodwill and respect that will facilitate the flow of communication for some time to come.

• **Overlook.** Pass around the praise whenever worthy goals are accomplished. Celebrate success and give every person his share of the spotlight. Failure to recognize the contributions of team players can diminish their willingness to go the extra mile. Give hard workers their due and then some.

• **Forget.** As each year passes, it is easy to forget what it was like to be young and inexperienced. Overly strict parents, unreasonable teachers, and unsympathetic bosses would do well to take a trip down memory lane and recall their own callow youth. The answer is not to set low standards but to offer more understanding, encouragement and support.

THINKING LIKE BARNABAS

1. Why is relationship the energizing core of the church?

2. Why is communication the heart of relationship?

3. How can health be affected by mere words?

4. How are words like a spark?

5. In what ways are discouraged people like house plants?

6. Why is it important to think twice before speaking?

7. What difference does it make if compliments are credible?

8. Explain how encouragers can praise creatively?

9. Why is it important for praise to be specific?

10. Do you prefer praise that is spoken or written? Explain why.

BEHAVING LIKE BARNABAS

1. Break into groups and, working from the list of 10 verbal responses that discourage the flow of communication, make a list of counter measures that will facilitate the flow of communication. Name some times when you are prone to be verbally discouraging and discuss how that cycle could be broken.

2. Pray for help to become more encouraging when talking to others.

3. This week's assignment is to encourage an elder. Shower him with praise.

Something that encouraged me last week was ...

Someone I encouraged last week was ...

To become more encouraging this week, I plan to ...

In the past week, I became more or less discouraging in these areas:

- Insensitivity   more / less   (critical, sarcastic, negative)

- Intimidation   more / less   (bossy, overbearing, threatening)

- Ignoring   more / less   (preoccupied, aloof, self-centered)

On a scale of 1 to 10, my use of encouragement skills during the past week was as follows:

- My mind   1 2 3 4 5 6 7 8 9 10
(thinking good, pure, positive thoughts)

- My eyes   1 2 3 4 5 6 7 8 9 10
(perceiving the good in every situation)

- My ears   1 2 3 4 5 6 7 8 9 10
(actively and enthusiastically listening)

- My lips   1 2 3 4 5 6 7 8 9 10
(verbally communicating respect and confidence)

- My hands   1 2 3 4 5 6 7 8 9 10
(sensing and acting on opportunities to do good)

I began each day asking for God's help to become a more encouraging person.
   Yes   No

The Hands of an Encourager

"There is no such thing as a 'self-made' man. ... Everyone who has ever done a kind deed for us, or spoken one word of encouragement to us has entered into the make-up of our character and of our thoughts, as well as our success."

GEORGE ADAMS

Words of encouragement are important, but by themselves, they are never enough to satisfy the needs of discouraged and hurting people. James and John renounced the concept of ministry in word alone.

> If a brother or sister is naked and destitute of daily food, and one of you says to them, "Depart in peace, be warmed and filled," but you do not give them the things which are needed for the body, what does it profit? Thus also faith [or encouragement] by itself, if it does not have works, is dead (James 2:15-17).

> By this we know love, because He laid down His life for us. And we also ought to lay down our lives for the brethren. But whoever has this world's goods, and sees his brother in need, and shuts up his heart from him, how does the love of God abide in him? My little children, let us not love [or encourage] in word or in tongue, but in deed and in truth (1 John 3:16-18).

The ministry of encouragement involves doing as well as talking. That is not to say active listening and verbal encouragement are not important or demanding. Listening empathetically and carefully selecting the right words to influence another person in a more positive, constructive and godly direction are crucial aspects of encouragement. Still, there is more. The crowning achievement of encouragement is learning to give yourself away in small deeds of kindness.

Benefits of Encouraging Deeds

Jesus taught His followers, "It is more blessed to give than to receive" (Acts 20:35). What are some of those blessings?

• *Friendships.* Givers are constantly making new friends who enrich their lives. They also improve existing ties by making regular deposits in their relational bank accounts. Steady deposits of love pay dividends more valuable than any financial institution can boast. Many conflicts between people can be traced to a person taking more out of a relationship than he is willing to put in. Just as surely as an ATM will reject attempts to overdraw an account, so will people who feel taken advantage of.

• *Adventure.* Another blessing enjoyed by givers is excitement and fun. Each day becomes an adventure as encouragers look for creative ways to bring smiles to their family and friends. There is no room for boredom when so many opportunities for giving abound.

• *Kindness.* Kindness benefits its bearer by activating the biblical law of reciprocity. Christians should do what is right regardless of the consequences, but Jesus and Paul never hesitated to use reward as an incentive for righteous behavior. Good works are not meritorious, but they do pay dividends.

> Give, and it will be given to you: good measure, pressed down, shaken together, and running over will be put into your bosom. For with the same measure that you use, it will be measured back to you (Luke 6:38).

> But this I say: He who sows sparingly will also reap sparingly, and he who sows bountifully will also reap bountifully (2 Corinthians 9:6).

Do not be deceived, God is not mocked; for whatever a man sows, that he will also reap. For he who sows to his flesh will of the flesh reap corruption, but he who sows to the Spirit will of the Spirit reap everlasting life. And let us not grow weary while doing good, for in due season we shall reap if we do not lose heart. Therefore, as we have opportunity, let us do good to all, especially to those who are of the household of faith (Galatians 6:7-10).

The law of sowing and reaping is unbreakable. The more one sows, the more he will reap. A random act of kindness will have its reward, but it cannot compare with the joy of making encouragement a way of life. Those who encourage bountifully are blessed bountifully.

• **Contagious.** When people respond in kind to human goodness, there is usually more than one beneficiary. The law of reciprocity starts a chain effect that touches the lives of countless people. Like tossing a stone into a pond, the ripples of encouragement are far reaching. It is intriguing to contemplate how one compassionate act will multiply itself over and over again. Kindness is contagious, and unsuspecting souls are encouraged every day as a result of something that happened previously between people unknown to them directly. Who knows where love can lead? Every day, Christians find encouragement in an event that took place 2,000 years ago.

• **Contentment.** Finally, giving produces the blessing of inner-peace. It just makes a person feel better. It is a blessing to contemplate the pleasure God takes in witnessing His children encouraging others through good deeds. Still, helping others live more courageously is its own reward. Human beings were created with a need to make a difference in other people's lives, and encouragement fills that innate desire.

It is hard for an individual to think about his problems while trying to minister to someone else. There is no room for discouragement in a mind filled with concern for improving the well-being of others. This alone should be sufficient incentive not to miss another opportunity to encourage.

Giving Is a Privilege

In light of Jesus' promises, giving is not a burden but a blessed privilege. It is ironic that self-centeredness never achieves what it longs for. The more one selfishly and obsessively seeks happiness, the more it eludes him. Real success in life is the difference between being useful and being a user.

The Bible is filled with tragic stories of shallow men and women who lived only for themselves. Ahab killed Naboth to possess his garden. Korah led a rebellion to acquire the high priesthood from Aaron. Absalom betrayed his own father to control the throne of Israel. Ananias and Saphira lied to the Holy Spirit for personal advantage. These takers live on in infamy, and their undoing was a foreshadowing of the sad consequences of selfishness.

The Bible also features names of noble men and women who died to themselves and lived their lives in service to others. These givers were abundantly blessed by God and are still admired today. Abraham gave his nephew Lot first choice of pasture land for his flocks. Prince Jonathan was ready to relinquish his claim to the throne for the good of the nation. Nehemiah gave up a comfortable life in Persia to provide political leadership for the reconstruction of Jerusalem. Paul counted all things loss for the excellency of the knowledge of Jesus Christ.

What a contrast. These well-known Bible characters stand as representatives at the head of two great groups which all men and women must choose between. The world has more than enough selfish people who engender ill-will, but givers make this planet a much better place to live. Givers endear themselves to others and establish a network of loving relationships while takers alienate people and have but one person on their team.

No one admires an indolent, miserly or gluttonous person. Those who are hungry for power or pleasure are pitied for their skewed sense of values. Those who are most respected are always the ones who make it their life's ambition to contribute to the happiness and well-being of their families and fellowman.

The Duty of Encouragement

Providing encouragement through thoughtful acts is unquestionably a privilege, but it is also a duty. Luke summarized Jesus' ministry by stating that He "went about doing good" (Acts 10:38). Because giving was the essence of the Savior's life, it is a holy habit to be cultivated by everyone who wears His name. "For we are His workmanship, created in Christ Jesus for good works, which God prepared beforehand that we should walk in them" (Ephesians 2:10). Saints are to be ready for every good work (2 Timothy 2:21; Titus 3:1).

An Eternal Investment

Christianity is more than sound doctrine and pious words. It is laying up treasure in heaven by investing in others' lives here on earth. This is something that can be done anywhere, anytime, by anyone. It is not necessary to be wealthy, brilliant, powerful or famous. All that is needed is a caring heart.

Encouraging others is one of the safest investments a person can ever make. No one can take away the grateful smiles and words of appreciation that are accumulated over a lifetime and stored in the heart. Some people collect coins, or spoons, or stamps or dolls, but an encourager collects something much more precious. What could be more satisfying than saving up memories of playing a small but significant role in providing the supportive context people need for making lasting positive changes in their lives.

Little Acts of Kindness

Giving is the heart of the gospel (John 3:16) and the true essence of living. But how should Christians give? People mistakenly believe that a gift must be expensive to be appreciated. Love cannot be purchased at a department store or a dealer showroom. Money and material possessions are often the least meaningful gifts. What people want and need is the time and attention of someone who cares for them. When love is withheld, gifts become empty apologies for a pattern of neglect. Presents cannot be substituted for presence.

Sadly, some assume that if a gift is big enough, it can make up for a lack of meaningful participation in the lives of those professed to be loved. Humans are obsessed with the big: big buildings, big business, big cars and big salaries. Everyone hopes to do big things in life. The only problem is that this kind of attitude can blind a person to the importance of little things. Little things to men may be big things in God's eyes. What really makes the world go round is ordinary people doing small tasks very well every day. Encouragers must never underestimate the power of small things.

If little things can be great things, how much more is that true when God is behind them? When the remnant returning from exile looked at the beginning of the new temple, they were disheartened. The prophet Zechariah scolded the people of Jerusalem for despising the day of small things (Zechariah 4:10). They felt they were too few and too feeble to build something of consequence, but Zechariah had news for them: "Not by might nor by power, but by My Spirit, Says the Lord of hosts" (Zechariah 4:6). The Jews failed to comprehend that God was working through them to accomplish His will. Christians who engage in the ministry of encouragement are also agents of God through whom He works to bless discouraged people.

The Test

One day, as crowds assembled to hear Jesus teach, He asked His disciples where they could buy bread to feed the multitudes (John 6:1-6). His question was merely a test. Jesus knew exactly what He was going to do. Philip was the first to respond, and without realizing the absurdity of his actions, he began to explain to the Lord why His request was economically unfeasible. His grade on Jesus' exam – an F.

Andrew, on the other hand, displayed a weak but obvious faith. Although he had no idea what Jesus would do, he went to work anyway. Finding a boy who was willing to share his lunch, he brought the five loaves and two fish to Jesus. Andrew must have felt embarrassed to present the Lord with his meager results, but, somehow, he knew it was the right thing to do. Jesus had the people sit on the green grass and, after blessing the food, multiplied it until more than 5,000 were fed. Andrew's grade – an A+. What lesson did Jesus want His followers to learn that day? The smallest effort is better than the greatest excuse.

How would you score on Jesus' test? Most people have a limited view of their ability to contribute to the lives of others in a meaningful way. God says, "Do not underestimate yourself. Your contribution may be small but what counts is your willingness to let Me work through you." This is the driving principle behind all worthwhile encouragement. Seemingly small acts can have a great impact on people's lives for good or evil.

Celebrate the Small

On the positive side, there is the Bible school teacher who dutifully fills her post each week encouraging children to follow Jesus faithfully. Dedicated husbands and wives, good citizens and faithful Christians are being forged in that little classroom although she may undervalue her efforts at the time. Or consider the saintly woman whose powerful prayers can move heaven to bless the sick, yet thinks she has little to offer the church. Who could underestimate the value of a simple note of encouragement to a bereaved widow. What price tag could be placed on a hug for a courageous brother who has publicly confessed his sin and desire for forgiveness. A home-cooked meal doesn't cost much, but it is a priceless display of Christian love. A hand sewn newborn's gown is inexpensive, but its value between friends is inestimable. The possibilities for encouragement are nearly endless.

Encouragement is leaving a fresh towel for the next person to shower. It is surrendering all rights to the remote control. It is leaving the closest parking space for a total stranger and the overstuffed recliner for your next of kin. It is watching another person eat the last piece of strawberry pie and enjoying it more than he did. It is happily washing dishes so that others can relax on the couch with the Sunday paper. It is making coffee and turning on the copier when you arrive at work first.

Encouragement is giving of self in small unheralded ways and loving every moment of it. It is basking in the pure delight of serving others. It is the pleasure of anonymity as a beneficiary of encouragement puzzles over the benefactor of his blessing. It is experiencing firsthand the joy of walking in the Spirit rather than the flesh (Galatians 5:16).

On the negative side, the opportunities to discourage are equally infinite. Discouraging tendencies may be innocent, but that does not render them harmless. No evil intent is required to inflict pain. Courtesy, cooperation and compliments withheld can be destructive in any setting. Being preoccupied, judgmental or aloof may not seem like earth-shattering events, but the damage done to relationships may be irreparable.

Real greatness comes from small acts of goodness performed daily by those who trust God to bless even mustard seed size efforts to encourage (Mark 11:23). The most important thing is simply to get started. Solomon urged, "Whatever your hand finds to do, do it with your might; for there is no work or device or knowledge or wisdom in the grave where you are going" (Ecclesiastes 9:10). Quit talking about it. Stop replacing action with incessant planning. Just get out there and do it.

10 Guidelines for Giving

1. *Value yourself.* Everyone has something worthwhile to give, and you are no exception (1 Corinthians 12:14). Accentuate your unique skills and talents.

2. *Don't barter.* Nothing is more repugnant than a gift with strings attached. Always give expecting nothing in return (Luke 14:14).

3. *Start early.* Get started the moment your feet hit the floor. Don't procrastinate or the day and its opportunities will slip by you (John 9:4).

4. *Begin at home.* Don't treat strangers better than your own family. Make home your encouragement laboratory and experiment freely (Luke 15:11-32).

5. *Act quickly.* When a warmhearted impulse hits you, act on it right then (Acts 24:25). Otherwise it will dissipate and a wondrous moment will be lost forever.

6. *Be alert* (John 9:39). Opportunities to encourage are nearly always present to the discerning eye. See with your heart and they will materialize around you.

7. *Enjoy giving.* Encouraging is one of life's greatest but most underappreciated pleasures. Savor the moment as God's gift to you (Philippians 4:4).

8. *Redeem time.* Too many precious minutes are wasted that could be put to good use (Ephesians 5:15-16). Take advantage of waiting rooms and long lines.

9. *Respect everyone.* Above everything else on earth, prize people, and treat the very least with the same dignity you would afford Jesus (Matthew 25:45).

10. *Think small.* Quit waiting to perform headline-grabbing heroics. Be practical, not pretentious. Seize the small!

THINKING LIKE BARNABAS

1. Why are words alone insufficient to fulfill the ministry of encouragement?

2. What are some of the blessings of giving?

3. How are relationships similar to bank accounts?

4. Why does self-centeredness seldom achieve the end it longs for?

5. Why are givers more admired than takers?

6. How is being an encourager like networking? How is it different?

7. Why are the most expensive gifts often the least meaningful?

8. What is the advantage of encouraging in small ways?

9. Why are people prone to undervalue small acts of kindness?

10. What advice would you give to someone wanting to be an encourager?

BEHAVING LIKE BARNABAS

1. Break into groups. Brainstorm ways to encourage others through small deeds of kindness. After 5 minutes, let each group read its list. Award one point for each group's unique ideas. Recognize the groups with the most points and the most creative idea. Type up a full list of everyone's ideas and distribute it at the next class period.

2. Ask God to help you fill your life with more thoughtfulness and kindness.

3. This week's assignment is to encourage a minister. Even he can use a lift.

Something that encouraged me last week was ...

Someone I encouraged last week was ...

To become more encouraging this week, I plan to ...

In the past week, I became more or less discouraging in these areas:

- *Insensitivity*   *more / less*   (*critical, sarcastic, negative*)

- *Intimidation*   *more / less*   (*bossy, overbearing, threatening*)

- *Ignoring*   *more / less*   (*preoccupied, aloof, self-centered*)

On a scale of 1 to 10, my use of encouragement skills during the past week was as follows:

- *My mind*   *1 2 3 4 5 6 7 8 9 10*
(*thinking good, pure, positive thoughts*)

- *My eyes*   *1 2 3 4 5 6 7 8 9 10*
(*perceiving the good in every situation*)

- *My ears*   *1 2 3 4 5 6 7 8 9 10*
(*actively and enthusiastically listening*)

- *My lips*   *1 2 3 4 5 6 7 8 9 10*
(*verbally communicating respect and confidence*)

- *My hands*   *1 2 3 4 5 6 7 8 9 10*
(*sensing and acting on opportunities to do good*)

I began each day asking for God's help to become a more encouraging person.
   Yes   *No*

The
Activity

of an
Encourager

Courage to Build:
Nehemiah

In this section of the book, we move beyond the inner workings of encouragement to the launchpad of our lives. It is not enough to understand the essence of encouragement or to grasp the skills essential to its success. Sooner or later, we must put our classroom knowledge to the test. We must begin practicing the proven principles of encouragement in our homes, churches, neighborhoods and businesses. It must be everyday and not just Sunday.

The purpose of the final four chapters of this book is to inspire you to action. The lines have been memorized and the dress rehearsal begins today. As you step out upon the stage of life, each new day affords you a fresh opportunity to improve upon your past performance. You will succeed because you have the courage to be imperfect, to learn from each mistake, and gradually to become the encourager God saw you could be even before He laid the foundations of the world.

As we look for motivation in our lives, the Bible provides the catalyst we need in the great stories of encouragement contained in its pages. It relates true accounts of men and women who developed a proficiency for helping others and who became champions of encouragement in their age. Not only will we look at human heroes to serve as our mentors, but also we will go to the archetype of encouragement, Jesus Christ, and to the unmoved first cause of all encouragement, God the Father. These are the masters, the connoisseurs, the virtuosos, the experts of encouragement who will provide the impetus we need to overcome the spiritual inertia that restricts our growth.

This lesson will shine the spotlight upon a man named Nehemiah who encouraged not an individual but a group of individuals. The dynamics of group encouragement involve the same basics discussed in previous chapters but applies them on a larger scale. It is the process of encouraging group cohesiveness to achieve shared goals. As group members learn how to relate more effectively with each other, their creative and productive energies are unleashed with the irresistible force of a bulldozer. Encouragers are spiritual earthmovers who empower people to change the landscape of their lives.

Dreams

The group Nehemiah hoped to inspire was the nation of Israel. It was not much of a nation by anyone's standards. After 70 years of living in exile, a small remnant of idealistic Jews made their way back to Jerusalem, their heads filled with lofty dreams of restoring the country's former grandeur. Everything went well until they arrived home, and their plans met head on with reality.

Dreams are much like children. Newlyweds excitedly long for the day when they can begin their own families. The thought of bringing a son or daughter into the world is exhilarating, almost intoxicating. Then one day the doctor confirms their suspicions and the giddiness is gone. A more sober form of happiness takes its place as responsibility weighs in.

There is a price to pay for giving birth to children or ideas. Morning sickness is a mother's first touchstone with reality. Physical nausea is accompanied by a different kind of queasiness when contemplating the life changes that lie ahead. Labor pain is the culmination of the body's commitment to birthing. Delivery, the finale of the womb, requires all of the body's parts to work in complete concert and with unmatched intensity. This vigorous, coordinated and painful effort is similar to the total commitment required of a group to actualize their aspirations. The joy that accompanies that moment of creation is like a mother's pride when she holds her newborn in her arms for the first time. All that was suffered becomes a vague memory, suppressed by the thrill of giving life.

Bearing a child is a snap compared to rearing one, and giving birth to a dream is nothing compared to sustaining it. It must be fed, changed and cuddled continuously. Without constant attention, its growth will be impaired, or it could even die. Many good ideas never reach their potential because they are abandoned or neglected at a young age. It is odd that society will refer to an innocent child fathered by an irresponsible man as illegitimate. Similarly, there are many legitimate ideas that received a bad name because someone walked away from them at the wrong time. Few things are more sad than an orphaned idea.

Dreams have formative stages that mimic a child's developmental years. From the "terrible twos" to the awkwardness of adolescence, they must be succored, supervised and supported. Anyone can conceive a child, but being a parent is the hard part. Similarly, visualizing a dream is easy compared to nurturing it. The difference is in the commitment. Parenting has always been the honorable part of giving birth whether to infants or ideas.

It was in a palace in the Persian capital of Shushan that Nehemiah conceived his dream. When the Jewish exiles first returned home, it was an exciting moment vicariously shared by their countrymen. Those who stayed behind longed for news on the success of the expedition. With few exceptions, the reports had been disappointing. It was thrilling when the foundation of the temple was laid shortly after the remnant's arrival in Jerusalem, but it was well over a decade before any serious attempt was made to complete the work. God raised up a dynamic duo of prophets to encourage the Israelites to finish the project. An older man by the name of Haggai was joined by a younger prophet named Zechariah, and together they challenged and inspired the nation to alter their priorities and rebuild God's house.

110 COURAGE TO BUILD: NEHEMIAH

Discouragement

Many years had passed since that high point. Jerusalem's progress was at a standstill and the crumbled ruins of the city walls were a constant reminder of their humiliation. If those walls could be rebuilt, it might be just the thing to restore the people's pride and confidence.

So what was the problem? Was the project too big? This was hardly the Great Wall of China. It had been done before, so surely it could be done again. What was the holdup?

The difference was discouragement. When the walls were first built, it was a time of growth and expansion. The people believed in themselves, their leadership and their God. They felt they could accomplish anything they set their minds to.

Now, hope and enthusiasm were in short supply. Israel had been crushed by the armies of Nebuchadnezzar, diminished by the shame and hardship of life in exile, and exhausted by the mere struggle to survive. Few things are more emotionally tiring than simply trying to keep one's head above water in the daily battle to exist. Sometimes, just getting by, just surviving can drain all the mental and physical energy a person or group has to give. The vision, idealism and unity of Israel were replaced by blindness, compromise and discord. It was every man for himself. Like the days of the judges, every man did what was right in his eyes.

Successful groups always stress teamwork over individuality. No general ever defeated an evenly matched army without coordinating his troops. No football team ever beat an opponent of equal talent without practicing together. The group that knows how to direct individual effort toward collective goals will always prevail over those who exhibit a "do your own thing" mentality. Each person has a unique and valuable contribution to make, but it is cooperation that makes the whole greater than the sum of its parts.

Nehemiah could see the discouragement of his countrymen all the way from Mesopotamia. He saw because he cared. All encouragement begins with compassion. It does not take a spiritual Sherlock Holmes to discover opportunities to help hurting people. Tenderheartedness is the womb of encouragement.

Determination

Nehemiah displayed the mind of an encourager when he linked thought with purpose and conceived the plan of reconstructing the city walls to wake Jerusalem's citizens from their self-pity and lethargy. If successful, the plan would jump-start the restoration of the nation. All some people would see was a public works project, but Nehemiah saw a new beginning with unlimited potential.

For many years, Nehemiah lingered in Persia, hoping that someone else would provide the motivational leadership lacking in his homeland. With each passing day, it became increasingly obvious that, if the job would get done, he was the man who would do it. The slogan of discouraged people is, "Why doesn't somebody do something?" The motto of encouragers is, "If not me, who?" and, "If not now, when?"

> And it came to pass in the month of Nisan, in the twentieth year of King Artaxerxes, when wine was before him, that I took the wine and gave it to the king. Now I had never been sad in his presence before. Therefore the king said to me, "Why is your face sad, since you are not sick? This is nothing but sorrow of heart." So I became dreadfully afraid, and said to the king, "May the king live forever. Why should my face not be sad, when the city, the place of my fathers' tombs, lies waste, and its gates are burned with fire?" Then the king said to me, "What do you request?" So I prayed to the God of heaven. And I said to the king, "If it pleases the king, and if your servant has found favor in your sight, I ask that you send me to Judah, to the city of my fathers' tombs, that I may rebuild it" (Nehemiah 2:1-5).

Having settled the matter in his heart, Nehemiah looked for an opportune time to broach the subject with the king. His moment came when Artaxerxes observed him deep in thought and inquired about his apparent mental distress. It was risky for any royal servant to show less than perfect contentedness in the presence of the king. Whether planned or inadvertent, a favorable outcome ensued. Following a silent burst of prayer, Nehemiah began to explain the humbling circumstances of his countrymen. This was the moment of truth separating

the cowardly from the courageous – the instant when a man must bold-
ly act on his dreams or retire forever to the comfort of the status quo.

Nehemiah had an influential position and a comfortable lifestyle.
Was he really ready to sacrifice his comfort and career to chase an il-
lusive goal? There was no promise things would work out as planned.
There was no guarantee his people would understand or appreciate
what he hoped to do. Dreams are risky business.

Fulfilled dreams have two parents: their father is courage and their
mother is faith. Too many people never give their most cherished dream
a chance to prove itself. Like overprotective parents, they lack confidence in its ability to measure up. They are so busy shielding it from
disappointment that they deprive it of any opportunity to succeed.
Like capable children, ideas need trust to show what they are made of.
Without the possibility of failure, there can be no growth, no ad-
vancement and no victory. Dreams are for the brave hearted.

Knowing his life would never be the same, Nehemiah began to
unfold his plan for rebuilding Jerusalem's walls and re-establishing it
as a regional power favorable to Persia. The king eagerly endorsed the
plan and promised his full support. There was no turning back now.
Come what may, Nehemiah would see it through to the end.

Encouragement requires personal sacrifice. Nehemiah gave up his
life in modern Shushan to become governor of a Third World country by the standards of his age. From a purely secular viewpoint, it
seemed a step down, but to an encourager, the opportunity to serve
others is always a step up because it is a step closer to God. The time
for words was over as Nehemiah embarked on one of the great encouragement adventures of all time.

Planning

> So I came to Jerusalem and was there three days. Then I
> arose in the night, I and a few men with me; I told no one
> what my God had put in my heart to do at Jerusalem; nor
> was there any animal with me, except the one on which I
> rode. And I went out by night through the Valley Gate to
> the Serpent Well and the Refuse Gate, and viewed the walls

of Jerusalem which were broken down and its gates which were burned with fire (Nehemiah 2:11-13).

For three days, Nehemiah collected information he needed to formulate a working plan for rebuilding Jerusalem's walls. On the third night, he conducted a first-hand survey of the situation. If he was to provide encouraging leadership for the men of the city, he would have to prove his worthiness. If he excited them with a flamboyant speech, but his plan proved shortsighted or impractical, it would be hard to recover their support. A good start was crucial to their success, and he was determined not to go off half-cocked. He did not need a perfect plan, but he did need a viable one. He could not anticipate every eventuality, but his attention to detail should demonstrate his thoroughness. Armed with a sensible approach to organizing the work, he proceeded to the next step.

Presentation

The time had come to meet with Jerusalem's leading men to win their support. An encouraging leader must identify and gain the confidence of a group's power base to succeed. Nehemiah hoped that somewhere in their hearts, their youthful dreams of rebuilding the city were still alive. If a small, smoldering lump of coal can be fanned into a roaring fire, then he was certain he could articulate a clear, compelling vision that would captivate their hearts and spark national renewal. Group encouragement requires a shared perception of a worthwhile and achievable goal. Inspiration is derived from the ability to conceptualize practical and positive change. Rebuilding the walls was unquestionably desirable and his plan was reasonable, but success ultimately hinged on their faith in his ability to lead. Nehemiah's careful planning, straight talk and contagious enthusiasm won him the support he needed.

Ardor without action is worthless, but passion is a powerful asset in the hands of a capable leader. Zeal cannot take the place of integrity, organization or hard work, but it can make the difference between success and failure when these prerequisites are met. Fervor is a major component in the ministry of encouragement.

Zeal is not inherently good or evil. Its benefit depends on the underlying cause with which it is associated (Galatians 4:17-18). Paul had a
misguided zeal that led him to persecute the church before his conversion (1:14; Philippians 3:6). The Israelites had a zeal for God but not
according to knowledge (Romans 10:2). In contrast, Nehemiah's devotion elicited God's favor and blessing. The Lord was pleased with his
mission and motive. Whenever people help others live more courageously, they are engaged in a good work. Ministers of encouragement
can be certain their labors have the approval and assistance of heaven.

Problem Solving

Responsibilities were delegated to foremen and laborers, and the
work was underway. Now came the tricky part: maintaining momen-
tum. Nehemiah knew that starting a project was always easier than
finishing one. His new job was to keep the ball rolling. Group encouragers understand problems are to be expected, and handling them
decisively and constructively is essential to success. The Jews faced
five stumbling blocks that could potentially cause a work stoppage:
criticism, hardship, discouragement, distraction and fear.

• **Criticism.** Criticism against the project surfaced immediately.
Men such as Sanballat and Tobiah used sarcasm and mockery to dishearten the workers. In times past, psychological warfare succeeded in
demoralizing the Jews, but that was before Nehemiah arrived on the
scene. Things were different now. His skill as an encourager helped
the people place criticism in proper perspective. No longer would they
be devastated by unjust criticism. No longer would they be controlled
by other's negative expectations. Because Nehemiah believed in them,
they began to believe in themselves. His words of confidence, approval
and exhortation kept the project on course.

• **Hardship.** Another difficulty was the hardship the work placed
on families who were already financially strapped. Famine had
stretched their resources to the limit, and it was difficult to keep their
minds on the work when money was so tight at home. High taxes and
exorbitant interest rates complicated matters further. These problems
were not directly related to building the walls, but they had an enormous impact on the laborers' ability to focus on their jobs and their

willingness to stick it out.

All projects are threatened by personal concerns that affect the lives of team members. Encouraging leaders are empathetic to real-life problems of those with whom they work. Group energy must not be drained by petty preoccupations, but there are legitimate concerns that ought not be ignored or trivialized. Groups are made up of living, breathing human beings, not robots. Nehemiah heard the people's concerns and intervened in their behalf to provide relief. He might have told them to leave their personal lives at home. Wisely, he chose a more compassionate tack, and the benefits to the work were immeasurable.

• **Discouragement.** Plain old vanilla discouragement also impeded their progress. Everyone is excited in the beginning of a venture, but after the newness wears off, dejection can take its place. Students who enthusiastically begin a new semester often feel overwhelmed when they reach the middle of the term. A young man's patriotic fervor may turn to depression halfway through boot camp. An idealistic woman who transfers to a new job will discover within a few months that her new company is not without its flaws. Passionate couples who gaze into each other's eyes as they exchange vows of devotion will soon realize that marriage is no fairy-tale cruise on the love boat.

Every enterprise enters a phase when idealism comes face to face with reality. Romantic notions give way to the hard facts of life. The experience may be gradual or abrupt, but, in either case, it is a real danger point. Encouragement is what keeps a student from dropping out, a soldier from going AWOL, a worker from job-hopping, or a couple from divorcing. Nehemiah helped dejected workers look beyond the rubbish at their feet to the final result. He reminded them of the importance of their work and the power of God to sustain their efforts. His words gave wavering workers the strength needed to keep on keeping on.

• **Distraction.** As progress on the walls continued, the opponents of rebuilding became increasingly desperate. They were no longer satisfied to hurl insults at their enemies. A conspiracy was formulated to destroy or discredit the movement's capable leader.

Nehemiah received an invitation to meet with Sanballat, Tobiah and Geshem in the plain of Ono. It was an honor that might easily have gone to Nehemiah's head. He could have mistaken their hospi-

tality for capitulation. Fortunately, Nehemiah sensed that something
was wrong and turned down the offer. His explanation was impressive:
"So I sent messengers to them, saying, 'I am doing a great work, so that
I cannot come down. Why should the work cease while I leave it
and go down to you?'" (Nehemiah 6:3). The offer was made repeatedly, but Nehemiah would not be moved by flattery or intimidation.

An open letter arrived accusing Nehemiah of rebuilding the city walls
to declare himself king. He was charged with masterminding a plot to
rebel against Persia. Unless he would come and clear up this matter, they
would be forced to inform Artaxerxes of his intentions. Nehemiah knew
the real purpose of the proposed meeting had nothing to do with as-
certaining the truth of the allegations because they were the ones who
fabricated the report. He refused to let petty politics bring his work to a
standstill. Any worthwhile undertaking will have its critics who impugn
the group's motives. Encouraging leaders must not allow themselves to
be distracted by critics who fear the erosion of their influence.

• **Fear.** The final attack came from a person Nehemiah trusted. The
greatest danger any project faces is from within. Brutus persuaded his
mentor Julius Caesar to attend the Roman senate on the day he was
murdered. It was one of Christ's own apostles who betrayed Him to
His enemies. In Nehemiah's case, the traitor was a professed prophet
by the name of Shemaiah. Shemaiah had been shut up in his house
presumably seeking a revelation from God on Nehemiah's behalf. The
governor was summoned to his house and informed that executioners
were on their way at that very minute to take his life. He was urged to
flee to the temple for safety.

Because the report was plausible and came from one professing concern for his safety, it must have caused Nehemiah great consterna-
tion. Later, it was discovered that the prophecy was a ruse designed
to discredit him, but on the night it was received, Nehemiah must
have feared for his life.

Nonetheless, Nehemiah feared something more than death, and
that was dishonor. If he fled into the temple and escaped with his life,
he knew his enemies would still gain an advantage by mocking his actions. He would be made to look weak and foolish, and his influence
would be diminished. If he could be panicked by rumor, imagine the

effect it would have upon skittish workers. He would rather die than disappoint, and observing his fearlessness kept them at their posts. His courage, in that desperate moment, preserved both his reputation and his dream. Men and women of God must act on their faith rather than their fears. Courageous leaders must stand on principle at all times, but especially during crisis.

Praise

The day finally arrived when the capstone was set in place, and the wall was complete. Yet Nehemiah knew his job was not finished. Future assignments remained to be tackled, and the people's willingness to get behind new undertakings would depend on their feelings about the previous project. The last step of any significant enterprise is to celebrate.

Celebration is an acknowledgment that the job was worthwhile and the participants' time well-spent. It is to applaud the impressiveness of the effort enabling the work to succeed. Affirmation and appreciation are essential to sustaining human endeavor. It is a huge mistake to underestimate the value of celebration because performance is directly connected to morale. Praising a job well done is important business, and no job is complete without it. Most of all, successful groups should stop and express thankfulness to God without whom their accomplishment would not have been possible.

In 52 days, the people of Jerusalem completed a project that eluded them for nearly a century. What was the difference but encouragement? The motivational principles that guided Nehemiah still work today. The challenge may be different, but the essentials of encouragement never change. Whether you lead a corporation, class, committee or clan, you can succeed by following these proven principles. Encouraging leaders are the wind beneath the wings of shared dreams.

Nehemiah's 10 Steps for Encouraging Groups

1. **Lean on God.** Attempting goals without God is like walking a tightrope without a net. An awareness of God's presence and sustaining power undergirds meaningful day-to-day activity. Underneath each project, each day and each life are God's everlasting arms. Tap into

His power through prayer.

2. **Identify needs.** Groups are encouraged when they understand how their objectives relate to satisfying real human needs. By clearly understanding the goal and its importance, cooperation is much easier to obtain. Life is about more than making money. Helping other people is inherently encouraging.

3. **Assess the situation.** Plans that are based on inadequate or inaccurate information are doomed before they begin. They just don't know it yet. Do your homework, and you will be ready for the final exam. Research, research, research.

4. **Make a detailed plan.** The difference between dreams and wishful thinking is in the details. People will judge your plans by their thoroughness and practicality. Think things all the way through and document relevant information. Don't take anything for granted.

5. **Articulate a compelling vision.** Encouragers understand the importance of the manner in which they present their ideas. Invest the time and energy necessary to make the right impression. Do more than state your goal. Help others envision it as you see it. Be clear but also be persuasive. Your enthusiasm will be catching.

6. **Delegate and organize.** Convey your trust in the integrity and competence of each group member. Do not discourage willing workers with vague expectations. Clarify all tasks and timetables. Provide ample training. Facilitate rather than dominate. Offer limited assistance but avoid micro-managing and taking over.

7. **Expect criticism.** Understand that it is impossible to please all people at the same time. Listen respectfully and take advantage of constructive advice, but do not waste time and energy trying to please impossible people.

8. **Resist distraction.** During any project, countless distractions can rob an individual or a group of its focus. Remember the tortoise and the hare and stay on track. Idleness, self-indulgence and over commitment are enemies of success.

9. **Follow-through.** Steadfastness is the most important ingredient for achieving group goals. The team that does not quit will reach its objective. When the newness wears off, discouragement will try to settle in. Remind group members of the importance of their work and

help them envision its completion.

10. *Celebrate.* Affirmation and appreciation satisfy basic human needs and are essential to sustaining human endeavor. Because the objective is complete, it is tempting to bypass this stage of group encouragement. To do so is shortsighted. Think of celebration as the first step of the next project you will undertake.

THINKING LIKE BARNABAS

1. How does group encouragement differ from encouraging an individual?

2. Can trying to do too many things at one time be discouraging?

3. How encouraging is the gift of cooperation?

4. How does an encourager's vision affect other group members?

5. How is giving birth to a dream like bearing a child?

6. How is sustaining a dream like rearing a child?

7. How important is it for a group to get off to a good start?

8. Are teamwork and individuality mutually exclusive?

9. With what kind of problems should encouraging leaders be prepared to deal?

10. Why is celebration important?

BEHAVING LIKE BARNABAS

1. Break into groups and make a list of possible solutions for dealing with a group member whose behavior is undermining the morale and performance of others.

2. Ask for God's help in becoming a more encouraging leader.

3. This week's assignment is to encourage a widow, young mother or shut-in.

Something that encouraged me last week was …

Someone I encouraged last week was …

To become more encouraging this week, I plan to …

In the past week, I became more or less discouraging in these areas:

- *Insensitivity*   *more / less*   (*critical, sarcastic, negative*)

- *Intimidation*   *more / less*   (*bossy, overbearing, threatening*)

- *Ignoring*   *more / less*   (*preoccupied, aloof, self-centered*)

On a scale of 1 to 10, my use of encouragement skills during the past week was as follows:

- *My mind*   *1 2 3 4 5 6 7 8 9 10*
(*thinking good, pure, positive thoughts*)

- *My eyes*   *1 2 3 4 5 6 7 8 9 10*
(*perceiving the good in every situation*)

- *My ears*   *1 2 3 4 5 6 7 8 9 10*
(*actively and enthusiastically listening*)

- *My lips*   *1 2 3 4 5 6 7 8 9 10*
(*verbally communicating respect and confidence*)

- *My hands*   *1 2 3 4 5 6 7 8 9 10*
(*sensing and acting on opportunities to do good*)

I began each day asking for God's help to become a more encouraging person.
   Yes   *No*

Courage to Bloom: Barnabas

"Never cease loving a person and never give up hope for him. For even the prodigal son who had fallen most low could still be saved."

SOREN KIERKEGAARD

Nothing in God's creation is more glorious than springtime as nature returns to life after a winter respite. Hues of crimson and violet explode across the countryside like fireworks on a fourth of July night. Yet nothing is more sad than a late frost. It marches south like Sherman's army spoiling scenic hillsides and prairies and leaving devastation in its wake. Flowering trees in parade dress, become casualties in the battle between seasons.

New Christians are like flowering plants in spring. Their faith is alive with breathtaking energy and enthusiasm. Their prayers are like a robin's song and the joy radiating from their faces is more vivid than a crab apple blossom. Yet just when their spiritual beauty is about to burgeon, youthful hope and ideals are cut short, nipped in the bud by discouragement.

Modern meteorology makes it possible to take preventive steps when frost threatens. However, it does not take an expert to forecast an assault on the faith of new converts. Satan will attempt to blanket their dreams with despair and render them useless before their spiritual lives ever begin to flourish. Like Florida farmers who mobilize to protect orange groves at risk, encouragers are triggered into heroic action when discouragement imperils believers whose tender faith is exposed to the elements of criticism and cynicism.

Barnabas was a master at motivating demoralized people and providing them with the courage to make their spiritual lives bloom. The name "Barnabas" literally means "son of encouragement," and never was a name more fitting. He was one of the earliest Christian converts. When the infant church began in Jerusalem, he sold his property to support the work. When Paul's fellowship was rejected by Christians in Jerusalem, Barnabas defended the genuineness of his conversion. Encouragement was a way of life for this man of faith, but never were his skills more needed or evident than when he encouraged the spiritual growth of a man named John Mark.

Making and encouraging disciples is the primary mission of the church (Matthew 28:18-20). Of all the good things a Christian may do, this is the most important. God commanded His people to approach this work aggressively and promised both His presence and power to help them succeed. To "make disciples" means to lead someone in learning about Christ and to assist him in becoming a mature follower of Jesus. In the case of Barnabas and John Mark, it involved three things: exerting influence, extending opportunity and restoring lost confidence.

Exerting Influence

> Then they all forsook Him and fled. Now a certain young man followed Him, having a linen cloth thrown around his naked body. And the young men laid hold of him, and he left the linen cloth and fled from them naked (Mark 14:50-52).

Only Mark records this interesting little incident. It appears unrelated to the main story unless tradition is correct in identifying the unnamed young man as the author himself. It was the custom of many first-century writers to remain anonymous, but vivid personal memories would frequently weave themselves into their work.

The clothing described appears to be some sort of night dress.

Perhaps the young man had been roused from his sleep by the noise taking place outside. His curiosity would be similar to someone hearing a siren emanating from his street today. When the soldiers attempted to arrest the young man, they may have mistaken him for an accessory to the band of "criminals" disturbing Jerusalem's peace with their radical teaching. In any case, he slipped out of their hands by shedding the loose fitting garment by which they held him. From this incident, and from all the talk about Jesus that was circulating throughout the excited city, it is obvious that Mark had an awareness of the Lord. Yet this was not enough. Many people know something of Jesus, but that does not make them disciples. More influence must be brought to bear to make that knowledge meaningful.

> And when Peter had come to himself, he said, "Now I know for certain that the Lord has sent His angel, and has delivered me from the hand of Herod and from all the expectation of the Jewish people." So, when he had considered this, he came to the house of Mary, the mother of John whose surname was Mark, where many were gathered together praying (Acts 12:11-12).

No where can influence be exerted for more good than in the home. The home of John Mark was an oasis of encouragement for both family and friends. Following the martyrdom of James, Peter was arrested and held in prison to stand trial. In the meantime, unceasing prayer was offered to God on his behalf. When Peter was delivered from prison by an angel, he went immediately to the house of Mary, the mother of John Mark.

Mary was a wealthy widow whose first love was her Lord. Her love for Jesus and His church was so fervent that she offered her home as a meeting place despite increasing danger. She was a woman with a deep belief in the power of prayer, and she and her friends prayed throughout the night for the apostle's safety. No doubt, her son was the subject of private prayer vigils on other occasions. No higher compliment could be paid to her faith than when Peter instinctively turned to her for sanctuary after his escape.

Just as Peter was sure where he could find welcome and refuge, there was no question in Mark's mind about what was important in his mother's life. The home John Mark knew was one where Christ was King. The immediate family affords life's greatest opportunities for encouragement, and Mary used them to the fullest.

In addition to the influence of his mother, Mark was encouraged through his friendship with Peter. In 1 Peter 5:13, the apostle referred to Mark as "my son." Those words indicate the existence of an intimate spiritual relationship. Some speculate that Peter was the one who led Mary and Mark to Christ. Behind every convert, there is someone who took a keen interest in his spiritual development. Eternal gratitude is due to that individual for a gift that can never be repaid. More important, every Christian needs to become that special someone in the life of another.

Mark was fortunate to be surrounded by many people of faith during his early years. Besides his mother and Peter, there was Barnabas who, according to Paul's letter to Colosse, was a cousin (Colossians 4:10). Kinship offers a unique opportunity to make a lasting difference in other's lives. It is widely known that most people who become Christians are influenced in their decision by someone related to them. Encouragers need to make full use of special ties with aunts, uncles, nieces, nephews and cousins. People connections are God's providential means of disseminating and perpetuating the faith once delivered unto the saints.

It is hard to overestimate the impressions left on Mark by these early influences. Barnabas, Peter and Mary each had a positive impact on the spiritual development of this young man. Similarly, modern encouragers can and must make effective use of their influence to help others live their lives more courageously and constructively. As plants must bud before they can bloom, so faith must sprout before it can spread.

Extending Opportunity

And Barnabas and Saul returned from Jerusalem when they had fulfilled their ministry, and they also took with them John whose surname was Mark. Now in the church

that was at Antioch there were certain prophets and teachers: Barnabas, Simeon who was called Niger, Lucius of
Cyrene, Manaen who had been brought up with Herod the
tetrarch, and Saul. As they ministered to the Lord and fasted, the Holy Spirit said, "Now separate to Me Barnabas
and Saul for the work to which I have called them." Then,
having fasted and prayed, and laid hands on them, they
sent them away. So, being sent out by the Holy Spirit, they
went down to Seleucia, and from there they sailed to
Cyprus. And when they arrived in Salamis, they preached
the word of God in the synagogues of the Jews. They also
had John as their assistant (Acts 12:25-13:5).

Barnabas was a model mentor. After completing business in Jerusalem, he and Paul took Mark back to Antioch to participate in the
exciting work going on there. It is one thing to lecture an intern, and
another thing altogether to show him the ropes. People always learn
more from doing than listening. Encouraging churches use appren-
ticeship programs to help new Christians spread their ministry wings.
Evangelism, youth work, visitation and teaching are just a few of the
areas where more mature Christians can help others gain the experience and confidence they need. Showing is better than telling.

To reach full bloom, a Christian must learn to love serving.
Beginning with the most humble duties, Mark graduated to more re-
sponsible tasks in the greatest world movement of all time. Had
Barnabas not seen Mark's potential and troubled himself to train
him, the church would have been much poorer. Those who were
converted through Mark's ministry owed a debt of gratitude to his
mentor. It must have been heartening for Barnabas to see his work
continued through the efforts of one he helped train. Nothing encourages like experience, and skilled encouragers seize every chance
to multiply their own usefulness by opening the door of opportunity for others.

Restoring Lost Confidence

Now when Paul and his party set sail from Paphos, they

came to Perga in Pamphylia; and John, departing from them, returned to Jerusalem (Acts 13:13).

At Perga John Mark took his hand from the plow and returned to Jerusalem. Why did he abandon the work and his friends? Everyone on that perilous journey faced the same difficulties, but only John Mark turned back. Why?

No explanation is offered in the biblical record, but there is no shortage of speculation. Perhaps the hazards of the journey were greater than he anticipated. Did he fear for his life? Could it be this rich kid was unaccustomed to hardship and longed for his old life of ease and comfort? Was he homesick for Mary or pining for a sweetheart? Mark's dereliction of duty may best be accounted for by his youth and immaturity. New Christians are especially susceptible to discouragement. In the beginning, there are struggles with problems that will pose little threat in later years.

Every disciple encounters his own Perga at some point. Christianity is joyous but also rigorous, and there is a moment in every saint's life when he asks, "Is it really worth it?" When a Christian feels like giving up, he is revisiting Perga.

Those who throw in the towel of faith will not find the happiness they were looking for when they return to their personal Jerusalem. After arriving home, it appears that Mark was thoroughly miserable. Perhaps he was disappointed in himself for failing to complete what he started. It must have been painful knowing that he let down men who were counting on him. Greater yet would be the thought of disappointing God who had done so much to bless his life. Hanging out with the guys could not have been the same anymore. The comforts of home he sorely missed must now have seemed trivial. One can only imagine how his conscience troubled him and refused to be quieted. One gets the sense that this young man was eager to return to the mission field and the purpose for which he was created.

All Christians make mistakes of one kind or another. The real concern is what to do about them. Dropping out of the Christian race is not an option. Neither is making peace with besetting sins. To make excuses for one's weakness is to own it and be owned by it.

One of the most critical functions of an encourager is to help disheartened people understand that mistakes are a part of maturing. The growth process involves many setbacks as well as advances. Courageous people are able see their reversals as part of life's curriculum for ultimate success. Rather than waving the white flag of defeat, they see an opportunity to advance from a different direction. Like great athletes, people of faith go through spiritual slumps, but they keep on swinging. When tackled short of their goals, they fall forward and get up again for the next play. One bad down in the game of life, does not spell defeat.

What some people call failure, others call experience. Reversals can be devastating, or they can be educational. Temporary setbacks spur courageous men and women to try harder and do better. Mistakes can be made to work for a person rather than becoming an excuse for spiritual collapse.

The recovery process involves several steps. It begins with a Christian owning up to his mistakes. Once a person has a self-encounter with honesty, he should take reasonable measures to make things right. After that, he should promise himself not to dwell on his regrets and drag himself down. Paul said, "one thing I do, forgetting those things which are behind and reaching forward to those things which are ahead, I press toward the goal for the prize of the upward call of God in Christ Jesus" (Philippians 3:13-14). In other words, do not live in the past. Whether that past is negative or positive is beside the point. Today is what counts.

Mark must have been embarrassed by his actions. He blew it, and no one was more aware of that fact than he was. Would his frostbitten zeal be cooled forever, or would he regain the confidence he lost and become a more effective servant for the experience?

> Then after some days Paul said to Barnabas, "Let us now go back and visit our brethren in every city where we have preached the word of the Lord, and see how they are doing." Now Barnabas was determined to take with them John called Mark. But Paul insisted that they should not take with them the one who had departed from them in Pamphylia, and had

not gone with them to the work. Then the contention became so sharp that they parted from one another. And so
Barnabas took Mark and sailed to Cyprus; but Paul chose
Silas and departed, being commended by the brethren to
the grace of God. And he went through Syria and Cilicia,
strengthening the churches (Acts 15:36-41).

After the success of their first missionary journey, Paul and Barnabas
decided to embark on a second venture. Their initial jubilation was
dampened as they began discussing the ministry team that would accompany them on this trip. Paul was dead set against taking Mark.
The cause was too important to entrust to unstable souls who might
bail out without notice. Paul insisted on using men whose character
was tested and proven.

Mark's ministry might have ended in that room had it not been
for Barnabas. He considered it unfair to hold one mistake over a young
man's head and brand him a quitter. Paul must have used all his persuasive powers to change his friend's mind, but nothing could weak-
en his support. Barnabas would stick by Mark.

Encouragement is an essential aspect of fulfilling the great com-
mission's mandate to make disciples. Everyone needs someone who
says "I believe in you." Everybody longs for someone who knows his
imperfections yet will stand by his side through thick and thin. Instead
of jumping on the bandwagon and belittling, encouragers defend.
Instead of shunning, they befriend. All people want encouragement,
but especially when they are down. When it was most needed, Barnabas
offered Mark forgiveness, acceptance, confidence and a second chance.
To his credit, he did not say, "Let's wait five or 10 years and see if he
proves himself first." Mark needed help right then, not at some vague
point in the future.

Some people refuse to forget the past even when sins were repent-
ed of long ago. Such an attitude could have destroyed Mark. It would
have been a blow to his self-esteem from which he might never have
recuperated. Thank God for men like Barnabas, sons of encouragement, whose faith in others has helped many modern Marks recover
their lost confidence. Encouragers are in the business of mending bro-

ken hearts and salvaging self-respect.

As a result of Barnabas' gritty determination to reclaim Mark, the young evangelist went on to accomplish great things. He became a dedicated missionary beginning with a trip he and Barnabas made to the island of Cyprus (Acts 15:39-41). His concise action-packed account of the life and ministry of Jesus was an effective tool in converting countless Romans.

Even Paul was convinced of Mark's usefulness in the end. In his letter to Philemon, Paul called Mark his fellow laborer (Philemon 24). In a letter to Timothy, he referred to him as useful (2 Timothy 4:11). The discouraged young man had become a first-class encourager to the great apostle himself.

The making of a disciple is not in the budding but in the blooming. It is not the start but the finish that counts. The process is not complete until life itself is complete (Revelation 2:10). That is why the church is so badly in need of men and women who make it their ministry to encourage others by exerting a positive influence, opening doors of opportunity, and helping fellow Christians triumph over disappointments and mistakes. You can nip discouragement in the bud by helping those around you to bloom. Make it your business to do all you can to assist others in fulfilling their spiritual potential.

THINKING LIKE BARNABAS

1. How is conversion like springtime?

2. How is discouragement like a late season frost?

3. How are encouragers similar to Florida orange growers?

4. Why is making disciples the most important of all Christian duties?

5. How should Christians exert their influence to encourage others?

6. How can Christians encourage others through extending opportunity?

7. Why did Mark leave the mission journey and return home?

8. How might Mark have felt after he arrived back in Jerusalem?

9. How important is it to have someone who believes in you?

10. What would have happened to Mark had it not been for Barnabas?

BEHAVING LIKE BARNABAS

1. Break into groups and assign these topics for discussion: What should encouraging Christians do when: 1) someone is baptized; 2) someone is restored; 3) someone quits attending services because he is disappointed in his behavior; 4) someone quits actively serving after being sharply criticized.

2. Ask God to help you become more encouraging to young people, new Christians and discouraged brethren.

3. This week's assignment is to encourage someone who is ill. Help bear another's burden.

Something that encouraged me last week was …

Someone I encouraged last week was …

To become more encouraging this week, I plan to …

In the past week, I became more or less discouraging in these areas:

- *Insensitivity*   *more / less*   (*critical, sarcastic, negative*)

- *Intimidation*   *more / less*   (*bossy, overbearing, threatening*)

- *Ignoring*   *more / less*   (*preoccupied, aloof, self-centered*)

On a scale of 1 to 10, my use of encouragement skills during the past week was as follows:

- *My mind*   *1 2 3 4 5 6 7 8 9 10*
(*thinking good, pure, positive thoughts*)

- *My eyes*   *1 2 3 4 5 6 7 8 9 10*
(*perceiving the good in every situation*)

- *My ears*   *1 2 3 4 5 6 7 8 9 10*
(*actively and enthusiastically listening*)

- *My lips*   *1 2 3 4 5 6 7 8 9 10*
(*verbally communicating respect and confidence*)

- *My hands*   *1 2 3 4 5 6 7 8 9 10*
(*sensing and acting on opportunities to do good*)

I began each day asking for God's help to become a more encouraging person.
   Yes   *No*

Courage to Believe: Jesus

"Life shrinks or expands in proportion to one's courage."

ANAIS NIN

One of the most common methods of diagnosing illness is a blood test. Blood is drawn from a patient and put under a microscope where it is closely examined. What is the doctor or medical technician looking for? They are searching for abnormalities, some departure from the healthful norm.

It seems that many people consider themselves society's personal medical team. They think it is incumbent upon them to examine everyone's speech, dress and actions. Quickly, they pass over good traits to focus on any flaw they can find. When a shortcoming is spotted, they magnify it out of proportion to reality. The final step is to spread the word to whoever will listen. Otherwise, some unsuspecting soul might pick up a strain of human imperfection through social contact with the "diseased."

But wait a minute. Is not every human being suffering from the sickness of sin? When Jesus was criticized for fraternizing with His patients, He responded, "Those who are well have no need of a physician, but those who are sick. I did not come to call the righteous, but sinners, to repentance" (Mark 2:17). Jesus told His interns to get a second opinion before going public with bulletins about the threat of epidemic from someone considered contagious (Matthew 18:15-17). The patient may have been misdiagnosed. He may be seriously ill but receptive to treatment. Quarantine is always a last resort.

The church is a spiritual center for disease control, but it does have standards – strict standards. Love, humility and consideration are at the core of the Christian's code of ethics. Perhaps it is time to unplug our microscopes and take a refresher course from the Great Physician whose methods are unexcelled in healing sin-sick people.

When Jesus examined His patients, He was fully aware of sin in their lives, but He chose not to focus there. Instead, He concentrated on the good and enlarged it. The adage, "What you see is what you get" is true, but what you see is determined by what you look for. Encouragers must adopt Jesus' habit of seeing the good. A review of some medical case studies will reveal how effective Jesus' methods of treatment were. By pulling the charts of Simon, Matthew and an adulterous woman, it will be demonstrated that encouragement is indeed good medicine.

Chart #1 - Simon

One of the two who heard John speak, and followed Him, was Andrew, Simon Peter's brother. He first found his own brother Simon, and said to him, "We have found the Messiah" (which is translated, the Christ). And he brought him to Jesus. Now when Jesus looked at him, He said, "You are Simon the son of Jonah. You shall be called Cephas" (which is translated, A Stone) (John 1:40-42).

It was Simon Peter's brother, Andrew, who first recommended Jesus to him. Andrew had been a "patient" of John the Baptist until he advised his followers that Jesus was more qualified to handle their cases. After a daylong consultation with Christ, Andrew was convinced. He could not wait to find his brother and share the good news.

Without an appointment, Andrew brought Simon Peter to meet Jesus, and the Great Physician worked him in for a free examination. Jesus looked at Simon but with far more than a passing glance.

Many people who beheld Simon were unimpressed with what they saw. He was a good-ole-boy: unstable, impulsive, rash. With penetrating eyes, Jesus looked into Simon's soul. He was a sick man, but the prognosis was good. "You are Simon the son of Jonah. You shall be called Cephas."

Cephas, Jesus' nickname for Simon, was an Aramaic term meaning "rock." Those who overheard the Lord must have questioned His assessment. How could He see rocklike qualities in someone like Simon? It was like calling a bald man "Curly" or a stout man "Slim." Others may have laughed to themselves, "He's hardheaded all right." But Jesus was talking about nothing less than Simon's character. He saw a man who would be steady in the face of duty and trial.

Was Jesus a quack? Was He deceived? Could He not see the faltering faith and broken promises of Simon? Did He not foresee that Simon would sink into the Sea of Galilee when his faith melted before the waves of a ferocious storm? Did He not know that Simon would deny and forsake Him in His most desperate hour?

Certainly Jesus saw all of this, but He also saw something else. He saw the day when He would gather His disciples at Caesarea Philippi and ask the question, "Who do you say that I am?" and that it would be Peter who made the grand confession, "You are the Christ, the Son of the Living God." He saw the time when His popularity would fade and multitudes of followers would leave Him, yet when asking His disciples if they too would depart, it was Peter who would reply, "Lord, to whom shall we go? You alone have the words of life."

When making His examination, Jesus did not confine His thoughts to what Simon was at that moment. He saw what he could be. He focused on his spiritual potential and challenged him to live up to it. Encouraging words are not idle chatter. They are inspiring, transforming words. Thanks to Jesus, Peter captured a new self-image and grew into its likeness.

On the Day of Pentecost after Christ's resurrection, Peter became the proud proclaimer of the first gospel sermon. When ordered not to teach or preach in the name of Jesus, his granite determination kept him from caving in to the Sanhedrin's pressure. In later years, he wrote letters encouraging saints to persevere in the midst of harrowing persecution. All of this because someone saw the good in him. One can only imagine the direction Peter's life would have taken without Jesus' words. Encouragement transformed him from a humble fisherman into a fisher of men.

Chart #2 - Matthew

> As Jesus passed on from there, He saw a man named Matthew sitting at the tax office. And He said to him, "Follow Me." So he arose and followed Him (Matthew 9:9).

The most unlikely candidate ever to become an apostle of Jesus Christ was a man by the name of Matthew. Matthew was a tax collector, and most people believed his occupation disqualified him from any association with respectable people. Few Americans have a warm feeling about the Internal Revenue Service, but dislike for this institution cannot compare with the hatred Jews had for their countrymen who collected money to support the occupying army of Rome. Publicans were considered the scum of society, and even thieves and murderers garnered more respect. Tax collectors were looked upon as traitors, political prostitutes, venal men who sold out their nation and whose loyalty could be bought.

Hard feelings were magnified by the manner in which taxes were assessed. The laws were vague and lent themselves to dishonest collection. Publicans frequently extorted money for their personal use, and there was little recourse for average people who sought justice. Those who protested at the tax office were met by the intimidating glare of a uniformed soldier stationed nearby.

The result was that most people begrudgingly paid their taxes, but those to whom they were paid became social outcasts. A publican was not welcome in the home of decent Jews, nor was he allowed in the synagogue. People would avoid him on the streets, whispering to each other and wearing looks that could kill. Perhaps the height of insult was that a tax collector's testimony was disallowed in Jewish courts. He lacked credibility as a witness because, in their minds, his occupation suggested he would say or do anything for profit.

One day, Jesus approached Matthew as he sat at the receipt of custom. Others had passed by his booth that day, and he felt their contemptuous stares. When Jesus looked at him, something was different. Matthew must have been taken aback by the pleasantness of Jesus' tone as He extended a most unexpected invitation: "Follow me" (Matthew 9:9). Matthew rose and left his office never to return again.

Matthew held a feast in Jesus' honor and used the opportunity to introduce his fellow publicans to the Savior. When the Pharisees learned what was happening, they asked His disciples, "Why does your Teacher eat with tax collectors and sinners?" When they looked at the banquet's guest list, they were repulsed. It shocked them that Jesus would mingle with such a disreputable group. In their minds, making an appearance at this gathering of sin-diseased men was the spiritual equivalent of attending a leper's convention.

Jesus was not blind. He too saw the spiritual sickness that filled the room where He feasted, yet He was not ready to write them off as terminal. A doctor who shuns his patients because they are ill is definitely in the wrong business.

Matthew emerged as one of Christ's most promising patients. Because Jesus saw something redeeming in him, he overcame the grip of materialism and devoted his life to sharing his newfound riches with others. As time passed, he used his pen to write a monumental defense of the gospel to his fellow countrymen. It is interesting to note that Matthew alone preserved a record of Jesus' greatest invitation: "Come to Me, all you who labor and are heavy laden, and I will give you rest" (Matthew 11:28). Those words held special meaning to an outcast such as Matthew. Perhaps to you as well.

Chart #3 - An Adulterous Woman

When Jesus had raised Himself up and saw no one but the woman, He said to her, "Woman, where are those accusers of yours? Has no one condemned you?" She said, "No one, Lord." And Jesus said to her, "Neither do I condemn you; go and sin no more" (John 8:10-11).

Jesus arrived at the temple early one morning to teach the crowds hungering for God's Word. His lesson was rudely interrupted by a group of Pharisees who brought a woman into the midst of His makeshift class. With all the piety they could muster, they declared, "Teacher, this woman was caught in adultery, in the very act. Now Moses, in the law, commanded us that such should be stoned. But what do You say?" (John 8:4-5).

From their words and manner, it was easy to tell that this shivering shell of a woman disgusted her accusers. When they looked at her, all they could see was her impurity. She was undeniably a wretched, dirty, soiled sinner, and they thought nothing of exposing her to public ridicule.

But what did Jesus see, and what did He say? Ignoring the Pharisees as if they had not spoken a word, He stooped down and wrote on the ground. Incensed, they became more demanding as they questioned Him a second time. Suddenly, they were silenced as Jesus lifted Himself up and calmly said, "He who is without sin among you, let him throw a stone at her first" (John 8:7). Convicted by the mysterious writing and their own unmistakable hypocrisy, they sheepishly exited one by one until Jesus and the woman stood alone in the crowd. When people really see themselves, they are able to look at others more kindly.

Too often, Bible school teachers spend an inordinate amount of time speculating about the message Jesus wrote on the ground. The real lesson is not what Jesus wrote but what He saw. Jesus saw something beautiful in this tarnished woman. As every person hung on His words, waiting even yet for His answer to the Pharisee's question, Jesus inquired, "Woman, where are those accusers of yours? Has no one condemned you?" She replied, "No one, Lord." Jesus said to her, "Neither do I condemn you; go and sin no more" (John 8:10-11). The Savior's words gave a despondent woman the courage she needed to change the course of her life.

"Go and sin no more." What did Jesus mean? Was He saying she was innocent of the charges against her? No, His words clearly implied she was guilty. Even she had not excused herself. Was He saying that adultery was a venial sin, of little importance to God? No, Jesus knew the heartache that a moment of unrestrained sexual gratification can produce. Countless broken homes, fatherless children and lost souls can be attributed to this so-called "victimless" crime between consenting adults.

Jesus was saying, "Things are not as hopeless as they seem. I know your past, but what matters is your future. I have looked into your heart and see a bright new tomorrow ahead of you. Your sins are forgiven and forgotten. Now, go and get started building a better life. You can do it. I believe in you."

Suddenly, an adulterous woman saw herself in a totally new light. Empowered by Jesus' faith in her, she was determined not to disappoint her Lord. Things would be different from that day forward.

It is interesting that the Pharisees could always find something in a person's life to complain about, even in the life of one who was sinless. When criticism becomes a habit, it is possible to see things that are not even there. How much better to live by the Golden Rule: "Therefore, whatever you want men to do to you, do also to them, for this is the Law and the Prophets" (Matthew 7:12).

No one wants to be put under a microscope. No one wants to be known and forever limited by his weakest moment. Everyone longs for someone who will see what is good and best in him. In fact, someone out there is waiting on you to show him his God-given potential and to mold him by your great expectations of his life. Someone is waiting right now for an encouraging word. Do not tear him down. Build him up. Never will you be more like Jesus than when you see the good in other people and help them to believe in themselves.

THINKING LIKE BARNABAS

1. How are critics like self-appointed physicians?

2. How is the church like a center for disease control? What are its standards?

3. What might people have thought when Jesus nicknamed Simon "Cephas"?

4. How difficult is it to look beyond the present moment in order to encourage?

5. How is it possible to encourage someone by molding his self-image?

6. How do you think Matthew felt when Jesus invited him to become His disciple?

7. When someone really sees himself, does he see others more kindly?

8. Why did Jesus choose not to condemn the adulterous woman?

9. Who saw your potential and challenged you to live up to it?

10. Name someone who is counting on you to see good in his or her life?

BEHAVING LIKE BARNABAS

1. Break into groups and see how many other people you can name that Jesus encouraged by seeing good in them.

2. Pray for God's help to look for and bring out the best in others.

3. This week's assignment is to encourage someone bereaved. Be very sensitive.

Something that encouraged me last week was …

Someone I encouraged last week was …

To become more encouraging this week, I plan to …

In the past week, I became more or less discouraging in these areas:

- Insensitivity   more / less   (critical, sarcastic, negative)

- Intimidation   more / less   (bossy, overbearing, threatening)

- Ignoring   more / less   (preoccupied, aloof, self-centered)

On a scale of 1 to 10, my use of encouragement skills during the past week was as follows:

- My mind   1 2 3 4 5 6 7 8 9 10
(thinking good, pure, positive thoughts)

- My eyes   1 2 3 4 5 6 7 8 9 10
(perceiving the good in every situation)

- My ears   1 2 3 4 5 6 7 8 9 10
(actively and enthusiastically listening)

- My lips   1 2 3 4 5 6 7 8 9 10
(verbally communicating respect and confidence)

- My hands   1 2 3 4 5 6 7 8 9 10
(sensing and acting on opportunities to do good)

I began each day asking for God's help to become a more encouraging person.
Yes   No

Courage to Battle:
God the Father

---

*"Life is a battle in which we fall from wounds
we receive in running away."*

WILLIAM L. SULLIVAN

Accurding to Aristotle (and Aquinas), every effect must have a cause.
If there is a contingent material world, then a noncontingent force
must have preceded it and brought it into being. The fact that the uni-
verse exists is compelling evidence for the existence of God.

Likewise, a planet that exhibits order and purpose must have an in-
telligent mind behind it. William Paley convincingly argued that
design demands a designer. It defies logic to conclude that the delicate
ecological balance sustaining life on earth is a product of chance.

Without cracking a smile, the evolutionist asks rational men and
women to believe that the earth and its inhabitants are but byprod-
ucts of gaseous material being ignited in a blast that scattered debris
throughout space. That explosion formed multitudes of galaxies and
solar systems, and at least one fortunate planet has evolved ever upward since that time.

Never mind that advocates of evolution can offer no sensible explanation for the origin of the gas that exploded or the matter that
was catapulted through the cosmos. Overlook the statistical impos-
sibility of a planet ordering itself into an inhabitable environment ca-

pable of sustaining life. Forget that they cannot account for the presence of living things other than to assert that they must have spontaneously generated because they are here. Disregard their inability to account for primordial life developing self-awareness, intelligence and creativity.

The truth is that the evolutionist's assertions will not stand up to serious investigation. Time and chance cannot account for the beautiful, orderly, life-filled planet we call home. In the beginning, there was God.

Going a step further, Immanuel Kant defended the existence of God based on man's sense of morality. How do you explain selfless service or heroic acts of bravery? Why would a person inconvenience himself or jeopardize his safety to help another? Cause and effect says that moral order in the world must be derived from a moral Creator. Love and compassion are not attributes of mindless matter. An eruption of atoms cannot account for honesty and integrity. Character and virtue attest to the holiness of the Heavenly Father. Kindness in the world can be traced back to a compassionate Creator.

What does all of this have to do with encouragement? Using the principles underlying classical apologetics, the existence of encouragement in this world demands the existence of an uncaused, first cause of all encouragement. The source of man's courage is an encouraging God. In times of trouble, it is comforting to know that the Great Encourager is always in. There is never a time when the Lord is unavailable or unwilling to impart courage to those who seek to honor Him with their lives.

The historical sections of the Bible faithfully record God's efforts to encourage His people in times of distress. That empowerment was especially evident in times of war. The Lord's encouragement gave Israel the boldness to withstand their enemies in battle. Ever since Abraham's skirmish against an aggressor named Chedorlaomer (Genesis 14:8-9), the people of God have been fighting the Lord's battles (Numbers 21:14; 1 Samuel 18:17).

Righteous nations do not view warfare as sport and are not instigators of hostility. Nevertheless, there are times when conflict is unavoidable, and people of faith must stand and be counted. They fight reluctantly but courageously for the preservation of their families. They find it regrettable but necessary to stop the unchecked advance of evil. The only thing more obscene than war is passiveness in the face of holocaust.

Warfare cannot be inherently evil because God is portrayed in Scripture as a man of war (Exodus 15:3; Psalm 24:8). He is the Lord of Hosts, a military designation similar to Commander in Chief (1 Samuel 1:3). He has ordered Israel's armies to attack, led them into battle, and fought by their side (Exodus 17:15-16; Numbers 31:3). On more than one occasion, the Lord revealed the proper time to launch an offensive campaign (Judges 20:18; 1 Kings 22:5; 1 Samuel 23:2-4; 30:8). Soldiers were considered His specially consecrated servants (Isaiah 13:3). Sacrifices were offered prior to the commencement of every campaign to secure His blessing (1 Samuel 7:8-10). His priests were commanded to accompany the army to the battlefield to exhort the troops.

> When you go out to battle against your enemies, and see horses and chariots and people more numerous than you, do not be afraid of them; for the Lord your God is with you, who brought you up from the land of Egypt. So it shall be, when you are on the verge of battle, that the priest shall approach and speak to the people. And he shall say to them, "Hear, O Israel: Today you are on the verge of battle with your enemies. Do not let your heart faint, do not be afraid, and do not tremble or be terrified because of them; for the Lord your God is He who goes with you, to fight for you against your enemies, to save you" (Deuteronomy 20:1-4).

Deborah and Jeremiah pronounced a curse upon cowardly Israelites who would not fight the Lord's battles (Judges 5:23; Jeremiah 48:10). The wilderness wandering was a direct result of Israel's unwillingness to follow God's instructions to wage war against the Canaanites (Numbers 14:1-12). The nation's noncompliance was not based on conscientious objections to war. They were simply too afraid to fight. Joshua and Caleb pleaded with their countrymen to trust in God's power to overcome their enemies. The faith and courage of this duo was

vindicated when, 40 years later, they conquered Canaan despite overwhelming odds against them.

The person who resists evil is not on the same level as his opponent. There is a world of difference between a patriot and a merce-
nary. Aggressors and those who withstand them are not morally equivalent. A police officer who carries a weapon is different from a crim-
inal who carries a gun. One is a law-breaker and the other is a law-
enforcer. One is a peace-officer and the other is disturbing the peace.
Whether the battle is between citizens of the same nation or coun-
tries in conflict, the contest between good and evil will continue until the end of time.

When hostilities erupt, God can be counted on to bolster the morale
of those who uphold justice. It is extremely difficult for a person to
perform his best when he is discouraged. That is why psychological
warfare is a major part of any military campaign. Disheartened troops
lose the will to fight and put up less resistance than those who believe
in their cause and their commander. There are many occasions when
the Lord took special measures to impart hope and courage to the
armies of Israel.

God Encouraged Moses

Israel's first battle was a struggle for independence. It was hard for a
ragtag group of slaves to believe they had any chance of gaining their
liberty from the mightiest military power on earth. God knew their
weakness and intervened on their behalf. Through a series of devastating plagues, He secured Israel's freedom. Still, Moses and the people were desperately in need of a boost in confidence. That necessity
was provided in a supernatural spectacle that accompanied the emi-
grants for the duration of their journey to the Promised Land.

As they departed from Egypt, a peculiar phenomenon appeared
in the sky capturing the attention of every Israelite – a cloud in the
peculiar shape of a column. The cloud did not lose its shape nor was
it moved by the wind. The peculiar column was more than a mete-
orological curiosity. It was a visible sign of God's presence.
Encouragement is a constant human need, and the billowy pillar would
go before them on their sojourn as a perpetual reminder of God's pow-

er to sustain them.

In the bright sunlight, the column looked cloudy, but at night, it gave off a fiery glow that could be seen from great distances. Like a flare, it illuminated the night sky and facilitated their travel. Its fire warmed their hearts with the assurance that God would watch over them day and night until they reached their destination (Exodus 13:21-22).

One of man's greatest fears is darkness. When the eyes cannot see, the imagination takes over and can fill the heart with terror. Every noise is a wild beast or a deranged attacker. The fiery pillar was like a great night light that kept Israel from stumbling in the dark, but it also kept their imaginations from running away with them. Similarly, encouragement can brighten a person's path and chase away imaginary fears that are incapacitating.

When the cloud went before them, Israel would strike camp and follow. With the precision of a compass, it kept them on course at all times. Likewise, encouragement helps people find their way and stay on track toward the fulfillment of their goals. Still, the magnificent pillar was more than a directional device. Ancient travelers used caravan fire to guide large groups. Iron grates with wood fires burning in them were attached to the end of long poles and carried in front of the company. In the daytime, the direction of the road was indicated by smoke, and at night, by the light of fire. The splendor of the pillar of cloud and fire was that it supplied courage as well as guidance. Perhaps its greatest benefit was simply reminding the people that they were not alone. Sometimes, the greatest encouragement a person can give is just being there for others in their time of need.

Shortly after releasing the Hebrews, Pharaoh regretted his decision and set out to recapture them. It must have struck fear into the hearts of the Hebrews when they learned they were being chased by the angry despot's chariot forces. They were unarmed, penned in and desperate. It was not a moment for the fainthearted. If ever a group of people needed encouragement, this was it.

Moses exhorted the people not to despair because the Lord Himself would fight for them (Exodus 14:14). When Moses stretched out his hand over the water, God parted the Red Sea opening a path to freedom between two enormous walls of water. Because the escape route was unmistakable, the pillar of cloud moved from the front of the company to the rear. Like a thick fog bank, it became a partition protecting them from their attackers. Encouragement, like the pillar of cloud and fire, can serve a dual purpose. Sometimes, it helps people move forward in a positive direction. At other times, it shields them from personal attacks. Encouragement can brighten a person's life or shelter him from blistering criticism.

When the last of the Israelites emerged from the dried sea basin, Moses passed his hand over the sea and the waters closed over the pursuers. The Israelites celebrated their freedom by praising God for His deliverance. Had it not been for His encouragement and intervention, they would be back in bondage. Today, encouragement enables people to free themselves from bondage to negativity and self-defeating habits that keep them enslaved. God is still deserving of praise for setting captives free from the tyranny of discouragement.

Israel faced many more battles before arriving in the Holy Land. They defeated the Amalekites at Rephidim (Exodus 17:8-16) and the great armies of Sihon and Og. In each engagement, the pillar of cloud and fire overshadowed them and supplied them with courage to fight with determination.

God Encouraged Joshua

Moses led Israel to the Promised Land, but his successor, Joshua, was to conquer and take possession of it. The Israelites were not selfish bullies pillaging for their own pleasure. They were God's instruments for restoring health and holiness to a region devastated by sin. Canaanite civilization had become so morally and spiritually corrupt that a holy God could not allow it to continue.

When the reigns of power were transferred to Joshua, the Lord spoke encouraging words to His new national leader. Completing his mission would require uncommon valor. Three times, the Lord exhorted him to be strong and courageous.

> No man shall be able to stand before you all the days of your life; as I was with Moses, so I will be with you. I will not leave you nor forsake you. Be strong and of good

courage, for to this people you shall divide as an inheritance the land which I swore to their fathers to give them. Only be strong and very courageous, that you may observe to do according to all the law which Moses My servant commanded you; do not turn from it to the right or to the left, that you may prosper wherever you go. This Book of the Law shall not depart from your mouth, but you shall meditate in it day and night, that you may observe to do according to all that is written in it. For then you will make your way prosperous, and then you will have good success. Have I not commanded you? Be strong and of good courage; do not be afraid, nor be dismayed, for the Lord your God is with you wherever you go (Joshua 1:5-9).

Future campaigns remained to be fought, and the Lord was a constant source of encouragement to Israel's army. Once they entered Canaan, the pillar of cloud and fire was gone, but God assured Joshua He would not fail him or forsake him. The removal of the visible manifestation of His presence did not mean He had departed. As He had been with Moses, so the Lord would be with Joshua.

In the battle against Jericho, God sent the commander of the heavenly host to personally brief Joshua on the plan of attack (Joshua 5:14). In the battle against Adoni-Zedek and his allies, the Lord hurled hailstones from the sky that claimed more casualties than those inflicted by Israelite army (10:11). As the enemy fled, God frustrated their escape by making the sun stand still (vv. 12-13). Unable to escape into the shadows of the night, they were decimated. Following a number of equally successful campaigns, the land was divided by lot, and the Israelites settled in to their new homeland.

The Lord continued to encourage Israel's army in future generations. Through a series of miracles, Gideon and his small band of 300 troops found the fortitude to take on an army numbering 135,000 (Judges 7:7). Believing God can save by few or many, Jonathan and his armor bearer, took the offensive against an entire outpost of Philistine soldiers (1 Samuel 14:6). Heartened by the sound of marching in the top of the Balsam trees, David engaged the Philistines at

Rephaim confident that the Lord's army had gone before him into battle (2 Samuel 5:23-24). Encouraged by Isaiah's prophecy, Hezekiah withstood Sennacherib's siege of Jerusalem until the Assyrians retreated after an angel of the Lord slew 185,000 enemy soldiers in one night (2 Kings 19:32-35). These are just a few examples demonstrating that those who put their faith in God find strength to sustain them in fighting life's battles.

God Encourages Christians

Christians are no less part of God's army than the men of ancient Israel. Paul called Epaphroditus and Archippus his fellow soldiers (Philippians 2:25; Philemon 1:2). When a person is baptized into Christ, he is immediately placed on active duty in the Lord's service. The church is an outpost of heaven on a mission of mercy to the oppressed and discouraged inhabitants of earth.

Paul explained the spiritual nature of Christian warfare in these words: "For the weapons of our warfare are not carnal but mighty in God for pulling down strongholds, casting down arguments and every high thing that exalts itself against the knowledge of God, bringing every thought into captivity to the obedience of Christ" (2 Corinthians 10:4-5). Because the battle is not carnal does not mean it is make-believe. In fact, the stakes have been raised. One group struggles for political freedom, but the other fights for spiritual freedom. One struggle is for time, but the other for eternity.

Christian warfare is more than an analogy. It is a life-and-death struggle for the souls of men, women and children. The enemy is real, cunning, powerful and determined. Paul warned, "For we do not wrestle against flesh and blood, but against principalities, against powers, against the rulers of the darkness of this age, against spiritual hosts of wickedness in the heavenly places" (Ephesians 6:12).

Although a Christian's weapons are not material, they are exceptionally powerful. Paul declared, "Therefore take up the whole armor of God, that you may be able to withstand in the evil day, and having done all, to stand (Ephesians 6:13). Where do Christians find the courage to stand and confront their fears? That kind of fortitude can only come from faith in God. The God who bolstered the courage of Moses, Joshua, Gideon, Jonathan, David and Hezekiah, will do no less for His people today. Soldiers of Christ must not run from battle. There are situations in life that must be faced squarely. Sometimes, the best way out of trouble is to confront it head on.

The Battle of Priorities

Christians must choose their battles carefully because some things are not worth the fight (2 Timothy 2:14). When is it appropriate for Christians to take a stand? No struggle is more perplexing than the war of priorities: "You therefore must endure hardship as a good soldier of Jesus Christ. No one engaged in warfare entangles himself with the affairs of this life, that he may please him who enlisted him as a soldier" (2 Timothy 2:3-4). The spiritual must come before the secular, and duty must come before pleasure.

Worldliness is not limited to wickedness. Christians may shun activities that are immoral and still be distracted from doing the Lord's will. It is possible for a person to over commit himself to good causes and neglect what is most important. Civic groups, charitable organizations and schools deserve the support of Christians, but the church must come first. The family must come before career and the spirit before the body. Rather than being obsessed with food, shelter and clothing, Christians must seek first the kingdom of God and His righteousness.

The Battle for Holiness

Spiritual people must also battle against lust. Peter wrote, "Beloved, I beg you as sojourners and pilgrims, abstain from fleshly lusts which war against the soul" (1 Peter 2:11). Even when a person desires to do right, he often struggles to act on his higher impulses. Paul explained, "For I delight in the law of God according to the inward man. But I see another law in my members, warring against the law of my mind, and bringing me into captivity to the law of sin which is in my members" (Romans 7:22-23). Cultivating a holy lifestyle is an arduous endeavor in which the lower nature must be subdued. When a person allows his sensual side to get the upper hand, it can ravage his relationships with God and man. James declared, "Where do wars and fights come from among you? Do they not come from your desires for pleasure that war in your members?" (James 4:1).

The battle for holiness is really a battle against selfishness. This struggle occurs within a man's own heart as his sensual and spiritual natures collide. No terms of peace can be made between these mortal enemies. It is a fight to the death. No where was this point better made than in the letter to the Galatians. In describing his new life, Paul declared, "I have been crucified with Christ; it is no longer I who live, but Christ lives in me; and the life which I now live in the flesh I live by faith in the Son of God, who loved me and gave Himself for me. ... But God forbid that I should boast except in the cross of our Lord Jesus Christ, by whom the world has been crucified to me, and I to the world" (Galatians 2:20; 6:14). Paul taught that this level of devotion is required of every loyal soldier in the Lord's army: "And those who are Christ's have crucified the flesh with its passions and desires" (5:24). Christians must put their God, and the good of others, before themselves.

The Battle for Sound Doctrine

Jude, the half brother of Jesus, wrote to Christians who were battling false teaching. He challenged them to "contend earnestly for the faith which was once for all delivered to the saints" (Jude 3). To contend means to strive as a combatant. Christians are to give their all in upholding the purity of the gospel.

False teachers were using God's grace to justify lascivious behavior. They defiled their bodies with immoral behavior and viciously attacked those who rebuked them. Anyone who dared to object was considered ignorant or intolerant. Every effort was made to turn the tide of public opinion against the proper leaders of the church.

Preaching is not a popularity contest, and doctrine cannot be determined by poll. Although controversy is unpleasant, spiritual patriots must be willing to defend the Bible's message from those who would distort it. When truth is under attack and souls are at stake, there is no place for pacifism. The battle must be fought and won. Still, contending for the faith does not imply rancor. It is essential to uphold the gospel with a Christlike spirit that demonstrates love for people as well as truth.

In any war there are major battles and minor skirmishes. Similarly, life consists of contests both big and small. In addition to weighty moral and doctrinal issues, there are more personal struggles that each person must face. Some saints struggle to lose weight, and others fight to gain weight. Some people suffer from shyness, and others wrestle with talking too much. Many people battle loneliness while others are desperate to find quiet time for solitude and meditation. Some people fight to free themselves from the grip of alcohol, tobacco, drugs and pornography, but numerous others battle addictions to television, chocolate, caffeine or golf. Some fight overcommitment while others work to conquer their inability to keep commitments. There are Christians who struggle with pride, and saints who battle low self-esteem. Those who strive to overcome what they consider to be deficiencies in their character will find God to be a source of unending encouragement.

At pivotal times throughout biblical history, God has intervened supernaturally to comfort and strengthen His followers. For Noah, He placed a rainbow in the sky. For Moses, it was the pillar of cloud and fire. For the apostles, it was Jesus' ascension into heaven. Every dream, vision and miracle was a means of imparting hope and courage to battle weary soldiers in the fight to triumph over unbelief and sin. How does God encourage His people today?

Worship as Encouragement

Worship is God's primary tool for imparting courage to His people. As God fills a Christian's cup, the blessings overflow into the lives of people with whom that person comes in contact. Paul praised God for this heavenly chain reaction: "Blessed be the God and Father of our Lord Jesus Christ, the Father of mercies and God of all comfort, who comforts us in all our tribulation, that we may be able to comfort those who are in any trouble, with the comfort with which we ourselves are comforted by God" (2 Corinthians 1:3-4).

Those who do not derive encouragement from worship are probably not worshiping in the way God instructed (John 4:24). Like the Pharisees, they have mentally crossed the obligation off their to-do list, but they might as well have stayed home for the good it did them. It is not enough to be physically present for the assemblies of the church. A person must also be psychologically or spiritually present. That is what Jesus meant when he said, "unless your righteousness exceeds the righteousness of the scribes and Pharisees, you will by no means enter the kingdom of heaven" (Matthew 5:20). Externalism is not enough. Something must happen on the inside. Forms of godliness lack power without the partnership of a willing spirit.

When the heart hungers for God, something special happens to a person who is worshiping. Each unique act becomes an avenue of blessing from God. Praying is encouraging because of God's assurance that He listens with unmatched intensity. He is never preoccupied or distracted. The Lord genuinely cares about the concerns of the petitioner and promises to providentially overrule in his behalf (Romans 8:28-39; 1 Peter 5:7). It is uplifting to contemplate the intercession of One whose perfect love is combined with infinite wisdom and limitless power.

Songs of praise are a poetic form of prayer that lift the heart into God's presence. The Lord's Supper empowers worshipers as they recall the depth of Christ's love and the certainty of His return. Sermons inspire Christians to live more courageously in view of God's promise to assist and reward them. Giving encourages worshipers by turning their attention away from self to the needs of others and the power of God to sustain those who put His Kingdom first in their lives.

Those who want to live truly courageous lives will not restrict their worship to corporate assemblies. Through private devotions, Christians can access the benefits of worship anytime they choose. No person can reach his spiritual potential without continually accessing God's power. Jesus' quiet moments of communion with the Father help to account for His undaunted courage. People who confine their petition and praise to one or two days a week are not serious about modeling their lives after Jesus.

Solitude and meditation are not the private domain of cloistered monks or professional ministers. In fact, beginners are often better at renewing their spiritual strength than many older Christians. The crucial factor is a longing for God (Psalm 42:1-2).

The greatest need of today's church is not smarter or more talented people. The single most important need is for courageous people who will live each day with a greater sense of God's presence and sustaining power. Devoted Christians are more than conquerors in the battle of life (Romans 8:37). As they personally triumph over fear and despair, they are transformed into ministers of encouragement dispensing faith, hope and joy to each person they meet.

Christians are members of a spiritual special forces unit whose mission is to encourage. This duty is not reserved for an elite contingent of the Lord's army. It is the responsibility of every faithful Christian. Every saint is to promote *esprit de corp* among the rank and file of his congregation. Every soldier is to extend hope to the community where he is stationed until recalled home to heaven.

Now that your basic training as an encourager is complete, it is time for you to take your place on the front-line in the battle against discouragement. God has promised to supply your every need. Be confident. Never lose hope. Victory is assured.

THINKING LIKE BARNABAS

1. Why do encouragers need encouragement?

2. Why does someone who is used to giving find it hard to depend on others?

3. How difficult would life be without the encouragement of fellowship?

4. Describe how you find encouragement through reading the word of God?

5. How does God encourage through prayer?

6. What do you find encouraging about the Lord's Supper?

7. How is singing hymns encouraging to you personally?

8. Why do you think God chose to encourage His people through preaching?

9. How does God encourage through meditation?

10. Which of God's promises is most encouraging to you?

BEHAVING LIKE BARNABAS

1. Break into groups and let each person share how he or she has benefitted from this quarter's study of encouragement. How do you plan to continue growing as a minister of encouragement?

2. Praise God as the encourager's all-sufficient power source.

3. This week's assignment is to encourage someone to study the Bible with you. God will give you the courage you need to complete this requirement. Lean on Him.

Something that encouraged me last week was ...

Someone I encouraged last week was ...

To become more encouraging this week, I plan to ...

In the past week, I became more or less discouraging in these areas:

- *Insensitivity*   more / less   (*critical, sarcastic, negative*)

- *Intimidation*   more / less   (*bossy, overbearing, threatening*)

- *Ignoring*   more / less   (*preoccupied, aloof, self-centered*)

On a scale of 1 to 10, my use of encouragement skills during the past week was as follows:

- *My mind*   1 2 3 4 5 6 7 8 9 10
(*thinking good, pure, positive thoughts*)

- *My eyes*   1 2 3 4 5 6 7 8 9 10
(*perceiving the good in every situation*)

- *My ears*   1 2 3 4 5 6 7 8 9 10
(*actively and enthusiastically listening*)

- *My lips*   1 2 3 4 5 6 7 8 9 10
(*verbally communicating respect and confidence*)

- *My hands*   1 2 3 4 5 6 7 8 9 10
(*sensing and acting on opportunities to do good*)

I began each day asking for God's help to become a more encouraging person.
   Yes   *No*

Afterword

> *"A word of encouragement during a failure is worth more than an hour of praise after success."*
>
> **Unknown**

B efore concluding, I wish to concede the imbalance of this book. I readily acknowledge that encouragement is not all pleasantries, and must, from time to time, entail uncomfortable but necessary intervention in the lives of those for whom one cares. Such acts of compassion are the highest evidence of Christian love and their performance requires great courage and sacrifice. All of this to say that there is much left to be written on the subject of encouragement and, Lord willing, I hope to offer a more well-rounded perspective on the subject in a subsequent work. In the meantime, it is my hope that this one-sided volume will help readers move a step in the right direction. May God providentially overrule the limitations of this book and use it for His glory and the betterment of His Church.

For Further Reading

> *"Correction does much, but encouragement does more. Encouragement after censure is as the sun after a shower."*
>
> Johann Wolfgang Von Goethe

Bolton, Robert. *People Skills.* New York: Simon and Schuster. First Touchstone ed., 1986.

Crabb, Larry. *Connecting.* Nashville: W Publishing Group, 1997.

Crabb, Larry and Dan Allender. *Encouragement.* Grand Rapids: Zondervan, 1990.

Dinkmeyer Sr., Don C. and Lewis E. Losconcy. *The Encouragement Book.* New York: Simon and Schuster, 1992.

Dinkmeyer Sr., Don C., Daniel G. Eckstein, and Dan Eckstein. *Leadership by Encouragement.* Boca Raton: Saint Lucie Press, 1995.

Dinkmeyer Sr., Don C., Don Dinkmeyer and Lewis E. Losony. *Skills of Encouragement.* Boca Raton: Saint Lucie Press, 1995.

Dunn, David. *Try Giving Yourself Away.* 3rd ed. Louisville: Updegraff Pr., 1998.

Fisher, Robert E. *Quick to Listen, Slow to Speak*. Carol Stream, Ill.: Tyndale House Publishers, 1990.

Getz, Gene A. *Encouraging One Another*. Chariot Victor Pub., 2002.

Swindoll, Charles. *Encourage Me*. Grand Rapids: Zondervan Publishing Co., 1995.